Crafting Phenomenological Research

Crafting
Phenomenological Research

Mark D. Vagle

Routledge
Taylor & Francis Group

LONDON AND NEW YORK

First published 2014 by Left Coast Press, Inc.

Published 2016 by Routledge
2 Park Square, Milton Park, Abingdon, Oxon OX14 4RN
711 Third Avenue, New York, NY 10017, USA

Routledge is an imprint of the Taylor & Francis Group, an informa business

Library of Congress Cataloging-in-Publication Data

Vagle, Mark D. (Mark Dennis)
    Crafting phenomenological research / Mark D. Vagle.
       pages cm
    Includes bibliographical references and index.
    ISBN 978-1-61132-301-6 (hardback : alk. paper) —
    ISBN 978-1-61132-302-3 (pbk. : alk. paper) —
    ISBN 978-1-61132-700-7 (consumer ebook)
    1. Phenomenology—Research—Methodology. 2. Social sciences—Research—
Methodology. 3. Education—Research—Methodology. I. Title.
    B829.5.V26 2014
    142'.7—dc23

                                                                    2013048331

Cover design by Jane Burton

ISBN 978-1-61132-301-6 hardback
ISBN 978-1-61132-302-3 paperback

For Nicole

Contents

Acknowledgments and Credits

Perhaps it can go without saying that writing a book, even when it is sole-authored, is never merely an individual act. There are many people who make it possible for the author to write and complete the endeavor.

It requires a supportive family—thank you Nicole, Maya, Rhys, and Chase Vagle for your patience throughout the process.

It requires an insightful, smart, and thoughtful publisher—which most certainly is how I would describe Mitch Allen. Thank you Mitch for providing such helpful feedback and guidance from early conception of this book through feedback and revisions.

It requires a production team with great eyes for detail. Ryan Harris at Left Coast and Jason Potter at Straight Creek Book Makers provided excellent copy-level and formatting support. Thanks to both of you.

It requires qualitative research scholars taking the time to read and respond to the manuscript. To Bettie St. Pierre, Madeleine Grumet, and Jim Scheurich, I deeply appreciate your endorsements of the book. To the anonymous reviewers, I extend my sincere gratitude for your time and generous feedback.

It requires someone to be willing to tend to tasks such as building the book's index—my thanks to University of Minnesota PhD student Angela Coffee for this.

It requires all sorts of people who help make the thinking and writing smarter. This includes, but is most definitely not limited to, colleagues and students who I have discussed, debated, shared, and learned Phenomenology with and from over the past 10 years. Most notably, I want to thank those colleagues and students at the Universities of Georgia and Minnesota. I cannot express how important it has been for me to engage in this learning with you. A special thanks to current and former students—Roberta Gardner, Brooke Hofsess, Hilary Hughes, Angel Pazurek, Joseph Pate, and Keri Valentine—whose work I highlight in the book.

And finally, it requires readers interested in engaging in these ideas. Thank you for being willing to see what this book might offer you. I sincerely hope you find it interesting and helpful as you navigate your crafting of phenomenological research.

Credits

Articles and Books

Freeman, M. and M. D. Vagle. 2013. "Grafting the intentional relation of hermeneutics and phenomenology in linguisticality." *Qualitative Inquiry* 19(9):725–735. Excerpts reprinted by permission of Sage Publications, Inc.

Gardner, R. "Reading race in a community space: A narrative post-intentional phenomenological exploration" (PhD diss., University of Georgia, 2013). Copyright © Roberta Gardner. Excerpts reprinted by permission of the copyright holder.

Hofsess, B. "Embodied intensities: Artist-teacher renewal in the swell and afterglow of aesthetic experiential play" (PhD diss., University of Georgia, 2013). Copyright © Brooke Hofsess. Excerpts reprinted by permission of the copyright holder.

Pate, J. "A Space for Connection: A Phenomenological Inquiry on Music Listening as Leisure" (PhD diss., University of Georgia, 2012). Copyright © Joseph Pate. Excerpts reprinted by permission of the copyright holder.

Pazurek, A. "A Phenomenological Investigation of Online Learners' Lived Experiences of Engagement" (PhD diss., University of Minnesota, 2013). Copyright © Angel Pazurek. Excerpts reprinted by permission of the copyright holder.

Vagle, M. D. 2009. "Validity as intended: 'Bursting forth toward' bridling in phenomenological research." *International Journal of Qualitative Studies in Education* 22(5):585–605. Excerpts reprinted by permission of Taylor & Francis Group. You can find other materials published by *International Journal of Qualitative Studies in Education* at the following website: http://www.tandfonline.com.

Vagle, M. D. 2010a. "Re-framing Schön's call for a phenomenology of practice: A post-intentional approach." *Reflective Practice: International and Multidisciplinary Perspectives* 11(3):393–407. Excerpts reprinted by permission of Taylor & Francis Group. You can find other materials published by *Reflective Practice: International and Multidisciplinary Perspectives* at the following website: http://www.tandfonline.com.

Vagle, M. D., H. E. Hughes, and D. J. Durbin. 2009. "Remaining skeptical: Bridling for and with one another." *Field Methods* 21(4):347–367. Excerpts reprinted by permission of Sage Publications, Inc.

Images

Original image for figure 2.2 from Chapter 2 in this volume used by permission of the copyright holder, Keri Valentine, Department of Career & Information Studies, Learning Design & Technology, the University of Georgia.

Introduction

> Phenomenology aims at gaining a deeper understanding of the nature or meaning of our everyday experiences … [it] does not offer us the possibility of effective theory with which we can now explain and/or control the world, but rather it offers us the possibility of plausible insights that bring us in more direct contact with the world. (van Manen 2001, 9)

Early in my doctoral coursework (March 2003) while participating in a Phenomenology colloquium, I recall Max van Manen—the visiting professor and renowned phenomenologist who led the colloquium—stressing something quite similar to what he had written a few years prior. Although I no longer remember the specific notes I wrote down in my notebook, nor the small-group conversation that followed, I do vividly remember how I found myself feeling, thinking, and being at that moment. I probably smiled.

I was experiencing a deep resonance—what van Manen would likely call a "phenomenological nod" (personal communication, March 7, 2003)—a time when one does not need to say "I understand," because one already knows one understands. I felt this way about phenomenology from the start, and even though plenty of folks have tried to talk me out of loving phenomenology—sometimes in subtle ways, and other times not so subtle—I have not obliged. Even when I was in the midst of being trained in my PhD program to question, interrogate, critique, test anything and everything, I found myself not wanting to do the same, in the same way at least, with this. I wanted to embrace it, hold it, much like I hold my children after being away from them for a few days. And the beauty of it was that I did not know why in a cognitive, logical sense. I knew it in my bones, in the fabric of my being and becoming. I felt this knowing.

It is this experience of knowing that constitutes phenomenology for me. That is, I believe my experience that day listening to Max van Manen was a *phenomenological encounter*—in that case with phenomenology itself. And I am confident that humans all over the world are having numerous phenomenological encounters each and every day of their lives. Some of these encounters might go unnoticed, others faintly recognized, and a few deeply felt—etched into our memories, our bodies, our beings, our identities.

This is the book's first core idea—*phenomenology is an encounter.* As you read, you will see numerous examples of phenomenological encounters—some taken from my life and the lives of my family; some from phenomenological studies I and others have conducted; some from popular media and art; and some from philosophers and human science researchers. In order to provide multiple and varied ways to engage with phenomenological encounters I have written the book using different types of textual forms. There is more traditional, scholarly prose, especially when I am discussing philosophical and methodological notions and principles, but also: poetry, works of art, storytelling, narratives, how-to checklists, comedic writings, and anecdotes, to name a few. I hope that this text is highly accessible for those interested in learning more about phenomenology, as well as for those who hope to live out their lives phenomenologically, since phenomenology, for me, is not only a philosophy and human science research methodology, but it is also and importantly, I think, a way of being, becoming, living, and moving through the world.

This is the book's second core idea—*phenomenology is a way of living*. It involves a deep and sincere commitment to, as phenomenological philosopher Robert Sokolowski (2000) suggests, *looking at what we usually look through*. It means trying to be profoundly present in our living—to leave no stone unturned; to slow down in order to open up; to dwell with our surroundings amidst the harried pace we may keep; to remain open; to know that there is "never, nothing" going on and that we can never grasp all that is going on; and to know that our living is always a never-ending work in progress (toward what is, of course, debatable). Because this idea can often seem abstract and elusive, I have explicitly tried to communicate this idea in a concrete manner throughout the book. I provide techniques, tools, strategies, and ideas to cultivate the notion of living a phenomenological life. These concrete writings often come in the form of examples, anecdotes, and exercises and are often visually represented in boxes as phenomenological encounters in order to draw and, I hope, keep your attention.

The book's third and most important core idea stems from and extends the "way of living" theme—*phenomenology is a craft*. It involves an embodied relation with the world and all things in it—and it is a creative act that cannot be mapped out in a once-and-for-all sort of way. The craft is practiced in many different ways and produces all sorts of different representations, and like other artistic forms, whether it be the visual, the theatrical, or the instrumental, sometimes what is produced tends toward the more linear, technical, and conventional, and at other times tends toward the more abstract, creative, and unconventional. In this way, the phenomenologist is continuously honing her craft, not simply learning steps to a methodological process and then carrying them out. This type of "craft work" takes time and care. Having conducted phenomenological research, theorized how to carry it out, read philosophical texts, and taught and mentored others about phenomenology, I feel that I am in an ongoing dialogue with this craft. It takes different shape each and every time I set out to design a study, read a philosophical idea, and respond to another's question, idea, wondering, and/or critique of phenomenology.

Perhaps the best way to illustrate what I mean here is to draw on something journalist Malcolm Gladwell explores in his book *What the Dog Saw: And Other Adventures*. In one chapter Gladwell writes about the concept of *amplitude* in sensory analysis, in this case taste. Based on his interest in learning more about how Heinz had cornered the market on ketchup, he had learned that amplitude was the measure for how all the discrete ingredients and the associated tastes combined, in their fullness, to give a food it's holistic, blended taste. Foods with high amplitudes, such as Heinz Ketchup, were often experienced differently than foods with low amplitudes. Even foods with basically the same discrete ingredients (referred to as component parts below) could taste very different from one another. To make this point more clearly, Gladwell's direct words are useful:

> After breaking the ketchup down into its component parts, the testers assessed the critical dimension of "amplitude," the word sensory experts use to describe flavors that are well-blended and balanced, that "bloom" in the mouth. "The difference between high and low amplitude is the difference between my son and a great pianist playing *Ode to Joy* on the piano," Chambers [Edgar Chambers IV, sensory expert and director of the sensory-analysis center at Kansas State University] says. "They are playing the same notes, but they blend better with the great pianist." (Gladwell 2009, 47)

I know we are not ketchup—and we may or may not be pianists. However, I think the metaphor is useful. I hope that as you work your way through this book—during your first read and subsequent readings and references to it in full or part over time—you find yourself practicing a craft that grows in its amplitude. This means that at times your phenomenology might sound more like Chambers' son on the piano than it does the concert pianist. This also means that you may want to focus deeply on a component part at one moment and another component part at another moment. This is all good. Learn the techniques and tools of the craft, give it a go—even if it feels awkward and clumsy. Please just keep going. Turn yourself over to the craft and see what comes of it. When starting out, try not to compare yourself to the high-amplitude Heinz ketchup phenomenologists, but do learn from these craftswomen and men. Discipline yourself to the time and care necessary to produce something interesting, important, and worthwhile. Hone your craft.

Navigating This Text

Guided by the themes of encounter, way of living, and craft, I have tried to write this text as an accessible narrative that is sequenced so that foundational philosophical issues, concerns, and assumptions are foregrounded (Section 1) and then applied to various ways in which phenomenology has been practiced in human science research (Section 2). I have tried to write it much like I teach it and practice it—as a dialogue around, through, and with ideas. I draw heavily on resources, assignments, and activities I have used in my phenomenology classes and public presentations—and have at times written as though I am presenting and responding to the questions/concerns/insights of others. At the same time, I have also tried to make sure this book in and of itself can serve as a resource of resources—which means that I provide examples, illustrations, and reflective commentary, as well as point you to other resources (See the *Resource Digs* at the end of each section and the *Additional Resources* section at the end of the book). Part of honing one's craft is to consider deeply all sorts of possible ways in which to practice the craft.

This point is consistently reinforced throughout the book. Phenomenology is not a singular, unified philosophy and methodology. When I teach and make presentations about phenomenology I often open with a statement something like, "If you leave here remembering only one thing, please remember that phenomenology is plural." I find it also important to emphasize that the sort of knowing *in my bones* that I referred to earlier has led me to read the philosophies of Edmund Husserl (German philosopher often referred to as the *father of phenomenology*), Martin Heidegger (Husserl's prized student who ended up leaving many of Husserl's ideas and putting hermeneutics and phenomenology in dynamic dialogue with one another), Maurice Merleau-Ponty (French philosopher who is credited for breaking down a mind-body dualism in phenomenological thinking), Jean-Paul Sartre (another French philosopher and social critic who deeply theorized the embodied nature of phenomenology), Hans-Georg Gadamer (a German philosopher who helped others see the limits of methods and brought language and linguisticality to the fore), and Gilles Deleuze (French post-structural philosopher who helps us see how concepts are entangled in complicated ways).

This kind of knowing has also led me to spend considerable time learning from others who practice phenomenology, others such as Max van Manen (Canadian phenomenological researcher operating out of hermeneutic traditions and the designer of a pedagogical phenomenology), Karin Dahlberg (a Swedish phenomenological researcher who designed a reflective lifeworld research approach), Amedeo Giorgi (a US phenomenological researcher operating out of Husserl's tradition and the designer of a widely used descriptive approach to phenomenological psychology), and Linda Finlay (a British phenomenologist who works across phenomenological philosophies and methodologies). I have come to a place with phenomenology such that I love it so much that I want and need to stretch its limits, re-imagine it, and put it in dialogue with other theories, philosophies, and methodologies—to see what it might become.

So, although I work my way through early or old phenomenology (as Ihde, 2003, calls it) in a pedagogical way, my heart and my growing craft is contained in the final section (Section 3) of the book—what I am calling *post-intentional phenomenology*. I say this here, now, so that my writing, and perhaps your reading, of the old phenomenology (i.e., the original philosophers mentioned above) is not interpreted as deficient. I do not see deficiencies, I see differences that have developed over time, as phenomenology has grown and changed. I think different types of phenomenology assume different things about what it is to know and be in the world. They adhere to different philosophical and methodological commitments, and serve different purposes. Again, I am deeply committed to laying out these differences, locating various possibilities these differences might afford, and pointing to those phenomenologists who write deeply about one or another approach to crafting phenomenological research.

To be clear, though, as I hone my craft as a phenomenologist I try to draw fewer lines of demarcation among ideas, concepts, theories, philosophies, and methodologies, and try to move across lines to see what might not be otherwise thinkable. I will make this more explicit in the final section of the book, but begin the book by drawing some lines, so that we can/might cross them later if we so choose.

Ready-ing Yourself for This Text

In order to sit with this text, I think it is helpful to start humbling ourselves now. What I mean by humbling is not the "aw shucks" kind of humility we perform when trying not to be boastful. Rather, I mean the kind of humility whereby we turn ourselves over to openness, wonder, and inquiry. It is the kind of humility we engage when we try to stop being so certain of what we know and think. It is the kind of humility evinced when we truly consider new things. It is the type of humility in which we let go.

Sometimes I like to use film to help myself and others slow down and let go. I have found the film *Peaceful Warrior* (Salva and Bernhardt 2006) to be particularly useful in this regard. It is about a gifted male gymnast who is a perfectionist, is very angry after suffering a major injury that puts his gymnastics career in question, and is struggling to let go of both his perfectionism and anger over his injury. Late one night at a gas station he encounters a wise man who practices Buddhism. Throughout the film we move with the gymnast on his journey toward peace and contentment. There are a number of moments in the film that I like to slow down and open up, such as a moment when the wise man is trying to show the gymnast that "there is never nothing going on." The paying attention, immediacy, and presence required to experience and practice *never-nothing-going-on* is significant. Experiencing this moment in that film can help provide some guidance toward how to embrace the openness that crafting phenomeno-logical research requires. If you have a moment, I encourage you to watch the film's trailer (http://www.youtube.com/watch?v=gegNMYvY_yg), or this excerpt (http://www.youtube.com/watch?v=bXAxBnQuHwI), or to consider viewing the film in its entirety.

Exploring Philosophical Concepts and Notions in Phenomenology

In this section of the book we will work our way through the following important questions:

1. What is a *phenomenon* in phenomenology? **(Chapter 1)**
2. What is *intentionality* and why is it so important in phenomenology? **(Chapter 2)**
3. How might *prepositions* help us grasp some of the philosophical nuances of phenomenology and put them to use methodologically? **(Chapter 3)**

In order to address these questions, I work across a number of philosophers and philosophical ideas in an attempt to emphasize aspects of phenomenological philosophies that I think are important to grasp in our crafting of phenomenological research. However, I do not come anywhere close to doing justice to the depth and complexities of these phenomenological philosophies. I strongly encourage you, as you continue to hone your craft, to be in dialogue with these philosophies. I learn new and incredibly important things each and every time I return to luminaries such as Husserl, Heidegger, Merleau-Ponty, Sartre, Gadamer, and Deleuze (to name a few). If I have learned anything in the last decade of studying philosophy within and outside phenomenology circles, it is that when we read and study philosophy, especially primary sources such as those listed above and especially if reading and studying philosophy is new to us, it is wise to remind ourselves of two things:

1. Philosophical texts are not written directly to us, as are many academic texts with which we might be accustomed. In this respect, philosophical texts might be, stylistically at least, more like novels. We are entering into ongoing dialogues/debates/arguments about ideas—philosophical in this case. We are not being told directly what something means or how it should be interpreted, nor are we provided guidance about what to "do" with the ideas. Turning ourselves over to this sense of journey and dwelling with ideas can free us up to engage in uncertainties.
2. Related, philosophical texts and the ideas therein are often not quickly and easily understood. They must be read and re-read, written about, discussed and debated. I have heard my former colleague Bettie St. Pierre at the University of Georgia (USA) urge others to let the texts "wash over" them. We are in pursuit of possible understandings and interpretations, not THE understanding. Turning ourselves over to ambiguities is also important.

With all this in mind, I have tried to capture some of the ideas important to phenomenology in an accessible way without oversimplifying complex matters. To do so, I share my own ongoing understandings, draw on contemporary philosophers who have also tried to write directly to the reader in an accessible manner (Dermot Moran and Robert Sokowloski in particular), and point to some of the ways high-amplitude phenomenological researchers such as Max van Manen, Karin Dahlberg, and Amedeo Giorgi use philosophical ideas to lay out their understandings of and preferred approaches to crafting phenomenological research.

While going to these sources yourself is necessary, I do hope that you will leave this section of the book feeling as though you have some sense of my interpretations of the philosophical ideas—particularly insofar as you are able to incorporate these ideas in your own unique crafting of phenomenological research and to engage in the never-ending complexities these ideas offer as your craft grows and changes in and over time. I also want to stress that I made some difficult choices about what to emphasize in this section. I erred on the side of "less is more" by foregrounding and privileging the notions of *phenomenon* and *intentionality* and backgrounding a number of other very important notions such as intuiting, intersubjectivity, lifeworld, phenomenological reduction, phenomenological and natural attitudes and immediacy. The latter are indeed discussed, but are woven through the central notions of phenomenon and intentionality in this chapter and are discussed in Section 2 as well.

My choices here are somewhat different than others who have written texts dealing with phenomenological research methods. Some spend time tracing key historical developments in the philosophy (e.g., van Manen 2001), others spend concerted time discussing the contributions of particular philosophers (e.g., Smith, Flowers, and Larkin 2009), and others do a bit of both (e.g., Dahlberg, Dahlberg, and Nystrom, 2008).

Again, I opted for the "less is more" principle, since one of the primary purposes of this book is to introduce researchers to phenomenological research, and in my teaching and presenting on this matter, students and others in attendance have often reported being overwhelmed by the sheer volume and complexity of the philosophy. One student said she had heard a seasoned qualitative research scholar lament that phenomenology is a turn-off because it is one of those research methodologies that takes so long to grasp that it is not worth doing. My sense is that this has a lot to do with the philosophical nature of phenomenological research. I have found that one way to help make the philosophy a bit less overwhelming—especially if/when one is new to philosophical writings—is to provide a few clear entry points into the philosophy, and then proceed deeper in and over time as we hone our craft.

That said, I think it is incredibly important to go deeper into the philosophy than I do in this section. What I provide here is a taste of some of the salient philosophical ideas. I strongly encourage you to turn to the sources I cite and to the Resource Dig at this end of the section. We begin with the primacy of phenomena in phenomenology.

CHAPTER ONE

What Is a Phenomenon in Phenomenology?

At its most basic level phenomenology, of course, is interested in the study of phenomena. Although many other quantitative, qualitative, and mixed methodologies also use the word phenomenon to describe the focus of their inquiry, phenomenological philosophers mean something very specific by phenomenon.

> The *phenomena* of phenomenology are to be understood in a deliberately broad sense as including all forms of appearing, showing, manifesting, making evident or "evidencing," bearing witness, truth-claiming, checking and verifying, including all forms of seeming, dissembling, occluding, obscuring, denying, and falsifying. (Moran and Mooney 2002, 5)

You might leave this quotation feeling quite confused—wondering what could possibly have not been included in this long list of -ing words. In order to break this down a bit, I find it most helpful to focus on two words in particular from this list—*manifesting* and *appearing*.

Phenomena Manifest

When German philosopher Martin Heidegger (1998 [1927]) described a phenomenon as *that which becomes manifest for us,* he was suggesting that phenomena are *brought into being* through our living in the world. Phenomena to phenomenologists, then, are not constructed, designed, or defined in the autonomously-encased human mind separated from the world, like French philosopher René Descartes had suggested centuries prior. Neither is it the case that they are unexplainable occurrences produced by outside forces. Rather, phenomena are the ways in which we find ourselves being in relation to the world through our day-to-day living. Therefore, the primary purpose of phenomenology as a research methodology stemming from its philosophical roots is to study what it is like as we *find-ourselves-being-in-relation-with others* (e.g., teacher with students, nurse with patient, therapist with client) and *other things* (e.g., a good book, some bad news, our favorite activity, an anxiety).

In this respect, phenomenologists do not tend to believe that humans construct a phenomenological experience. When humans experience the world they, again, *find themselves in* the experience. The verb *find* is not meant to signal an archaeological excavation of meaning, but a careful, reflexive, contemplative examination of how it is to BE in the world. Some of Sartre's words provide a helpful theoretical image (Moran and Mooney 2002):

> To know is to 'burst toward' to tear oneself out of the moist gastric intimacy, veering out there beyond oneself, out there near the tree and yet beyond it, for the tree escapes me and repulses me, and I can no more lose myself in the tree than it can dissolve itself in me. I'm beyond it: it's beyond me ... Knowledge, or pure "representation," is only one of the possible forms of my consciousness "of" this tree; I can also love it, fear it, hate it, and this surpassing of conscious-ness by itself that is called "intentionality" finds itself again in fear, hatred, and love. Hating another is just a way of bursting forth toward him. (Moran and Mooney 2002, 382–3)

I discuss the philosophical concept of intentionality in Chapter 2. The important point here is to understand that phenomenologists, for example, are not primarily interested in what humans decide, but rather in how they experience their decision-making. For instance, as one makes a difficult decision, how does one find her- or himself? In pain? Satisfaction? Confu-sion? Clarity? Sartre makes an important distinction for those trying to figure out how phenomenology can be of use. Phenomenologists are not interested in trying to represent the qualitative properties of the tree (i.e., its shape, texture, colors). Rather, phenomenologists are interested in how one finds him- or herself in relation to the tree. How is it to experience the tree? Perhaps the tree is a big oak in which one spent her or his childhood building a tree fort, swinging from a tree swing, having picnics, taking naps with grandma or grandpa. The tree, then, is not just part of what Husserl referred to as the *natural world* when he was articulating the need for a focus on the *lived world,* replete with a trunk, limbs, branches, leaves, and roots. It has lived, felt, and sensed significance. The child, now as an adult, has particular relations with the tree. When coming back to this old oak tree, how the adult found-herself-in-relation-with the tree often is brought back into being. Phenomenologists are interested in these sorts of phenomena.

Phenomena Appear

> The term "phenomenology" is a compound of the Greek words *phainomenon* and *logos*. It signifies the activity of giving an account, giving a *logos*, of various phe-nomena, of the various ways in which things can appear. (Sokolowski 2000, 13)

Extending Sokolowski's point here, it is important to understand that phenomena can appear in innumerable ways—and to say that some-thing appears rather than is built inside one's mind is saying something, philosophically speaking, quite important. Sokolowski stresses that the significance of phenomenology as a philosophical movement resides in how it helped Western thought get out of what he terms its *egocentric predicament*[1]—namely, that Descartes had created a subject-object (mind-world) dualism that had served as the dominant philosophical discourse in Western thought for hundreds of years. For Descartes, consciousness resided in the human mind; hence, meanings were thought to have been created in the mind, separate from the public and social sphere. In this sense, one could not theorize or make sense of appearances because each human mind was locked unto itself. In Descartes's way of thinking, appearances were merely creations in the mind and could not really, then, be thought of as real, living, and moving in and through the world.

> For phenomenology, there are no "mere" appearances, and nothing is "just" an appearance. Appearances are real; they belong to being. Things do show up. Phenomenology allows us to recognize and to restore the world that seemed to have been lost when we were locked into our own internal world by philosophical confusions. Things that had been declared to be merely psychological are now found to be ontological, part of the being of things. Pictures, words, symbols, perceived objects, states of affairs, other minds, laws, and social conventions are all acknowledged as truly there, as sharing in being and as capable of appearing according to their own proper style. (Sokolowski 2000, 15)

When we study something phenomenologically, we are not trying to get inside other people's minds. Rather, we are trying to contemplate and theorize the various ways things manifest and appear in and through our being in the world. The sooner we can grasp this the better. As I will explain more fully in Section 2, the influence of Descartes's (often referred to as Cartesian) philosophy remains strong—especially its privileging of an autonomous meaning-making agent, an individual human mind, as well as a world constituted by the mathematical sciences, and an objective world. Phenomenologists are not trying to join chemists, biologists, mathematicians, and physicists in finding more precise ways to explain how things work. Phenomenologists are interested in trying to slow down and open up how things are experienced, as scientists, theologians, students, teachers, nurses, leaders, bricklayers, electricians, plumbers, mechanics, and so on, are doing what they do. Phenomenologists want to study the lifeworld, as Husserl discussed—that is, the world as it is lived, not the world as it measured, transformed, represented, correlated, categorized, compared, and broken down.

In this way, phenomenologists set out to study how things are being and becoming—not how individuals construct things nor how the mathematical sciences represent things. This also means that phenomenologists do not assume that any one individual's experiences of some "thing" wholly belongs to that individual in any sort of final or idealized way. The philosophical assumption is that the individual is being, becoming, and moving through the lifeworld in intersubjective relationships with others and with intentional relationships with other things. The phenomenologist, then, is not studying the individual but is studying how a particular phenomenon manifests and appears in the lifeworld. Particular individual humans might help the phenomenologist gain important access to all sorts of important manifestations and appearances of the phenomenon, but the "unit of analysis" in phenomenology is the phenomenon, not the individual.

I have found that often the philosophical explanations of *phenomena* in phenomenology can begin to become more accessible through autobiographical accounts or anecdotes prompted by film. I often encourage others, especially when they are not sure of the phenomenon they want to study or whether what they want to study "is" a phenomenon (phenomenologically speaking), to spend time with movies. There are three concrete reasons I think this can be helpful when identifying a phenomenon of interest.

1. Film, much like the novel, takes us on journeys of meaning, interpretation, insight, thought, and feeling. We are not told directly what we are to understand—rather we enter into dialogic relations with phenomena. Sometimes we relate directly, other times not. However, we do find ourselves in relation with important aspects of the lifeworld. We are not asked to control and test these aspects. Rather, we are asked to live them a bit with the characters, plot, setting, etc.
2. Films, then, are saturated with manifestations and appearances. Around each and every turn we are able to experience all sorts of manifestations and appearances, some seemingly central to the film, others fairly minor or perhaps unrelated. In phenomenology, though, there are no more or less important manifestations. Each and every manifestation holds equal and great promise of putting us in contact with something incredibly deep and rich about living in the world.
3. The filmmaker, like the phenomenological craftsperson, does not get to decide what might manifest or appear for the viewer/reader. The viewer/reader enters into a dialogic relationship with the outcome of the phenomenologist's or filmmaker's craftwork and innumerable manifestations and appearances become thinkable.

When approaching a film with the goal of identifying potential phenomena for study, I am not necessarily "studying" the film. I am actually trying to experience the film more openly and deeply. Every now and then a manifestation strikes me in a particular way—it makes me think and feel deeply. It is at these moments that I try to pay better attention and to become a bit more contemplative. During the writing of this book I had one such experience that I now share.

Phenomenological Encounter #1
Manifestations and Appearances via Film

I recently watched the movie, Admission (Weitz and Croner 2013), on a flight from Atlanta, Georgia to Salt Lake City, Utah. The movie stars Tina Fey, who plays an accomplished admissions counselor at Princeton University working feverishly to become the director of admissions. One of the key themes in the story centers on each applicant's skill at figuring out how to apply—how to position oneself to be successful and how to package one's application for success. As one might predict, Princeton's company line is that there is no "secret" to gaining admission—however, the students being considered had incredibly high GPAs, SAT scores, and had been extremely active in extra-curricular activities.

For all sorts of reasons that I will not spoil for you here, Fey's character becomes interested in making sure one particular applicant is admitted. Perhaps predictably, this applicant's character is written as coming from a working-class upbringing[2] and, therefore, as a person without the social capital required to know how to position himself properly for Princeton. Also predictably, his character is written as a genius and who is in it for the love of learning and not people-pleasing or legacy-building or capitalist-reproducing. This last point is emphasized by his passionate, anti-establishment teacher (played by Paul Rudd) as the long-shot applicant enters his interview with a notable Princeton alum. Rudd's character makes a special effort to emphasize the applicant's true love for learning, that he will not sell out to anything less than a quest for knowledge and understanding, etc. Even though Rudd's character's advocacy here made perfect and predictable sense given how his character had been developed throughout the film, I still felt their awkwardness as he and the applicant realized that he had simply made things worse. However, what resonated the deepest with me was one single look and pause from the Princeton alum. It was a pause and look of judgment, power, and evaluation. The Princeton alum may have followed with some condescending language just after the pause and look. But he did not need to. His words were quickly lost on me, as I immediately found myself less present with the film and more present with the first time I applied for a doctoral program—just after my Master's degree, before I became a school administrator, long before I knew what it might mean to get a doctorate and well before it was even thinkable to consider becoming a professor. I could feel the manifestation of something(s) coming—and although I am not sure that the particular manifestation(s) I write about in the poem below will ever grow into a phenomenological study, I am confident that there are phenomena present and that they could be studied phenomenologically.

* *

Not Yet . . .

Want a doctorate
Why?
Not really sure. I have always held this as a goal.
Why?
I want to be able to be an effective educational leader.
Ok. So what are you interested in studying?
Umm . . . well . . . how leaders affect what happens in schools.
What do you like to read?
Yes, umm, yes, my Miller's Analogies Scores weren't very good (Why did I say that?).
Tell us about that.
I guess it's because, my vocabulary is, well, I guess it 's because I haven't read a lot of really difficult texts—I mean it's not what I do in my leisure time, I mean I read for particular purposes. . . . I didn't grow up reading difficult texts. I grew up in a really small town, and I guess I wasn't surrounded by . . . I guess I need to work on that.
So, what do you like to read in your leisure time?
Well, again, I read for particular purposes, to accomplish goals, and tasks and once in awhile read a John Grisham novel.
That pause.
That look.
(They don't want me . . . I am not ready . . . I can't do this . . .)
Not Yet . . .
Driving away, knowing I failed
Pit in my stomach, grows to a tightening in my throat
If only I had been more . . . careful
More certain, more polished
More scholarly, more refined
Not Yet . . .
Feeling ashamed, knowing I failed
Wondering why I lacked confidence
Why I mentioned my test scores
My vocabulary
Feel small, very small
Like my small town
Not Yet . . .
Growing angry and deeply sad, knowing I failed
Pretending I didn't really want it
That it wasn't necessary
Defending where I was from
Despising who I wanted to become
Not Yet . . .

* *

Four years later I was admitted into a doctoral program and have since read more "challenging texts" than I can count. I now sit in judgment of others like me—wanting to be accepted into a doctoral program, wanting to pass preliminary exams, wanting to successfully defend dissertations. I wonder what pauses and looks I enact, embody, and give.

The point here, in this book, is not to resolve these matters. Rather, it is to illustrate how phenomena are circulating and showing themselves around every corner—one 30-second segment in one film can provide us with openings to potential phenomena to explore. We just need to pay attention.

CHAPTER TWO

What Is Intentionality and Why Is It Important?

Much like their conception of phenomena, phenomenologists use the word *intentionality* to mean the inseparable connectedness between subjects (that is, human beings) and objects (that is, all other things, animate and inanimate, and ideas) in the world. This choice of words poses problems as the root word *intention,* especially in vernacular American English, often signifies one's purpose or rationale for doing something. The first task, then, is to release ourselves from this understanding of intentionality and embrace a philosophical understanding of intentionality. The use of intentionality here does not mean what we choose or plan. It is not used to signify any action we might want to take. It is used to signify how we are meaningfully connected to the world.

When one studies something phenomenologically, one is studying a phenomenon and the intentional relations that manifest and appear. One is studying *how* people are connected meaningfully with the things of the world. People might be connected to other people (e.g., teachers, caregivers, leaders), places, and hobbies in many different ways. Depending on the "object" of their intentional relations, the intentional relationships might manifest as confusion, respect, despair, hope, resistance, being in love, to name a few. It is these sorts of phenomenon that phenomenological philosophers were referring to when they wrote of intentionality.

Intentionality as Interconnectedness

A colleague and I (Freeman and Vagle 2009) have argued that much of the confusion regarding intentionality in US thought lies in the pervasive assumption that people act as autonomous meaning-making agents oriented to the world with purpose and intent.

Merleau-Ponty (1964 [1947]) describes intentionality as the invisible thread that connects humans to their surroundings meaningfully whether they are conscious of that connection or not. Sartre has described intentionality as the ways in which we meaningfully find ourselves "bursting forth toward" the world (Moran and Mooney 2002, 383). Regardless of how it is described, intentionality is a difficult concept to grasp. Part of its confusion lies in the strength of the image of the autonomous meaning-making agent orienting to the world with purpose and intent.... Intentionality is neither in consciousness nor in the world. It is the meaning link people have to the world in which they find themselves. People in their everyday contact with the world bring into being intentionality but not in the sense of choice or intent. (p. 3)

Interestingly, some of the students in my phenomenology courses from Eastern countries such as China, Japan, and South Korea have found the Western conception of intentionality to be quite similar to the notions of *interconnectedness* and *unity* in philosophies such as Buddhism and Taoism. They seemed to feel that the notion of human's interconnectedness with the world is a given. In other words, it seemed curious that Western philosophy did not give interconnectedness the same primacy. This speaks, in part at least, to the emphasis given to the individual ego in Western societies. That is, consciousness has been conceived as something that resides *in* humans and not between humans and the world. We will now slow down here and open up where consciousness "resides" in phenomenological philosophy.

Phenomenologists have consistently and stubbornly asserted that consciousness is always *of* something (Sokolowski 2000), as opposed to consciousness being conscious in and of itself. Sokolowski stresses that, although today this point seems obvious, it is necessary to continually assert it. In many of the dominant European philosophies that preceded phenomenology—for example those produced by Descartes, Hobbes, and Locke—Sokolowski reminds us of their presumption that when we are conscious we are "primarily aware of ourselves or our own ideas. Consciousness is taken to be like a bubble or an enclosed cabinet; the mind comes in a box" (Sokolowski, 2000, 9). In this way, it became assumed that our ideas and experience are directed inwardly rather than toward the outside. The assumption then, prior to phenomenology, was that "our consciousness, first and foremost, is not 'of' anything at all" (p. 9). It was as though consciousness existed without any direct reference to the "things" of which we could be conscious.

Phenomenology has tried to pull humans out of this egocentric predicament and into the intentional relations that always already exist. This is one reason why I am particularly fond of Sartre's *bursting forth toward* image of intentionality (Moran and Mooney 2002). The active energy does precisely the pushing that is necessary. For lack of a better phrase, Western philosophy has needed, and continues to need to get out of its own head—and out into the interconnectedness of human relations among human beings and with the things of the world.

Intentionality as Essencing

At the same time, phenomenology itself, broadly conceived, has been critiqued by qualitative researchers for its focus on *essence*—that is, on the view that there is an essential structure to a phenomenon and the intentional relations that characterize that phenomenon. The primary assumption is that phenomenological philosophers and researchers must be interested in determining universal truths that transcend time and space and which are also unaffected by social context, power, and agency. Athough at first glance this concern appears justified, I think that in order to make sense of concerns about essence and its relationship to social context, etc., it is necessary to return to the philosophy for guidance before and as we are crafting phenomenological research.

Although Husserl was interested in creating a new philosophical foundation for the human sciences, I think his thoughts about essence have been conflated with the notion of *essentializing* and lead qualitative researchers to picture the final outcome of phenomenological research as the identification of an *essential core*. Indeed, Husserl was interested in what he called "turning to the things themselves," rather than arriving at subjective meanings, objective meanings, or predictive and explanatory theoretical explanations of human experience. The "things" Husserl referred to, however, were the intentional meanings that presented themselves (manifested, appeared) in human consciousness through lived experience. By essence, Husserl was signaling that these "things themselves" had essential qualities that made them that particular thing and not something else. For instance, when people experienced love, they were not experiencing hate or resentment—and they most certainly "knew" and "lived" the difference. And for Husserl, love had essences that could be described along a horizon of meanings that was ever-expanding (Dahlberg 2006). Really then, Husserl's essence was not about finalizing anything but capturing what makes something like love what it is for humans in their intentional relations with one another and with the world.

Reconceiving Intentionality through Images

Even with this interpretation of Husserl's uses of "essence" in mind, the negative connotations associated with that word are mighty strong. The word carries so much baggage that it is difficult to convince skeptics otherwise. Personally, I have become less interested in defending essence and more interested in re-imagining phenomenology by putting phenomenological philosophies in dialogue with aspects of post-structural philosophies. In order to be clear about how the philosophical concept of intentionality takes different shapes in different types of phenomenological research, I emphasize some key distinctions.

1. If you are planning to craft phenomenological research following in the approach established by Husserl and Transcendental Phenomenology,

I suggest you spend time with the idea of *essence*. From a philosophical, theoretical, and methodological-coherence standpoint, the way intentionality is conceived in phenomenological approaches that follow Husserl involves a search for the essence of the intentional relation of a particular phenomenon. In this type of phenomenological research, intentionality is assumed to have essential structures or qualities.

2. However, in Heideggerian or hermeneutic phenomenology there is a different assumption. I argue that when Heidegger (1998 [1927]) broke away from Husserl's reliance on consciousness in favor of more ontological (being-in-the-world) explanations, new possibilities emerged. As discussed in Chapter 1, for Heidegger, the root *phenomenon* in phenomenology meant *that which becomes manifest for us.* In this conception, phenomenology becomes more about manifestations than about essences. From a hermeneutic perspective, such manifestations *come into being* through intentional relations, which are always already being interpreted. Intentional relations, then, are in a constant state of interpretation—and logically there would not necessarily be an "essence" of a phenomenon, but plausible interpretations of manifestations and appearances.

3. In post-intentional phenomenology,[1] I go a step further in saying that whatever understanding is opened up through an investigation will always move with and through the researcher's intentional relationships with the phenomenon—not simply in the researcher, in the participants, in the text, or in their power positions, but in the dynamic intentional relationships that tie participants, the researcher, the produced text, and their positionalities together. In this way, intentionality is always moving, is unstable and therefore can be read *post-structurally.* I do not add the word *post* to this research approach to mean "after" intentionality—as though it is time to progress beyond intentionality. Rather, I bring particular aspects of post-structural work to bear in phenomenological research. For instance, I am drawn to something St. Pierre (1997, 366) stresses in her description of fieldwork as *nomadic inquiry* and think that it has much to offer phenomenological researchers. "A consolation derived from an authentic, stable essence is no more possible in places than in subjectivities. Both are performances accomplished within relations, and both, for the sake of ethics, require persistent critique." If one is to persistently critique such performances, one must come to grips with the reality that he or she is always already positioned in particular places at particular moments in time—and I argue that this positioning is only known through intentionality. Studying intentional relationships also resembles what Lather says about validity in qualitative research—that "it is not a matter of looking harder or more closely, but of seeing what frames our seeing" (1993,

675). In this way, the intentional "findings" of phenomenological research are de-centered as *multiple, partial, and endlessly deferred*. A post-intentional phenomenological research approach resists a stable intentionality, yet still embraces intentionality as ways of being that run through human relations with the world and one another.

Combining Heidegger's manifestations, the philosophical notion of intentionality, and post-structural commitments to knowledge always already being tentative and never complete, I have created a *tentative manifestations* image that can be juxtaposed with images of an essential core (Husserlian)[2] and a spiraled hermeneutic circle (Heideggerian).

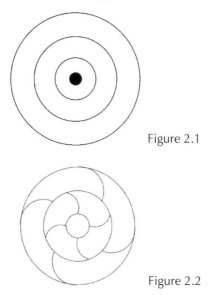

Figure 2.1

Figure 2.2

Figure 2.1 (essential core) signifies an "extreme case" in that it is designed to represent the common critique of phenomenology described above. Figure 2.2 (hermeneutic spiral) signifies how interpreted meanings are always in motion, and that these meanings circulate. In this way, we are entering into a dialogue with these meanings, rather than describing an essence of these meanings. Figure 2.3 (tentative manifestations) signifies a post-intentional move away from essence and toward contexts, situations, and the partial. Figure 2.1 can be read as layers of an onion peeled away until one finds the essential core—as the critique seems to assume. In Figure 2.2 there are no layers to peel, just an ever-circulating motion that can come back to, remake, do, and undo itself. In Figure 2.3 the lines can be read as flexible and malleable and, although not visible here, permeable. In Figure 2.1 the core is stable and singular. In Figure 2.2, there is no core, just multiple meanings

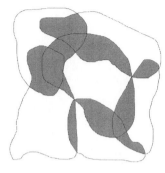

Figure 2.3

always already in motion. And in Figure 2.3 the points of overlap in grey are multiple and more temporary. If the figure could be set in motion the malleable lines would move and shift, as would the points of overlap. As will be described more fully in section 3, if we craft a post-intentional text we are elucidating these grey areas, the tentative manifestations—not trying to center the meaning.

Regardless of the particular approach you take in crafting phenomenological research, it is critical to clearly articulate how you conceive of intentionality, intended meanings, and intentional relationships. In my courses I have asked students to write *phenomenology briefs*. The idea is to help students write clearly and concisely about the philosophical concept of intentionality and connect it directly to a phenomenon of interest. I have found it to be a worthwhile and helpful exercise for those learning the craft because it helps them keep the philosophy and the methodology connected.

Phenomenological Encounter #2
The Phenomenology Brief

You will write a phenomenology brief (2-3 pages, single-spaced). The brief will include the following components:

1. A statement of what you take *intentionality* to mean, drawing on at least one philosopher to help you make your case.
2. A discussion of how your understanding of intentionality can be used to examine a particular phenomenon of interest.

How Might this Be Structured

Option #1 (Two Distinct Sections)

Section 1: Discussion of intentionality. Write it as a step-by-step explanation, balancing your interpretations with direct excerpts. Conclude this section with a concrete idea or quote that you can use in section 2.

Section 2: Begin by clearly stating a phenomenon of interest in your life, field, area of research, etc. Then describe how your intentionality, described in Section 1, can help you study, learn more about, understand more fully this phenomenon.

Option #2 (Weaving)

You can begin the brief with either the phenomenon or intentionality and then move back and forth between the two throughout the entire paper. It is still good to have some type of opening statement that sets up the reader—so be sure to provide something concrete to get the reader "readied" for what you are going to walk them through. Like option #1, you should balance your interpretations with direct excerpts throughout the brief.

Option #3 (Pushing the Bounds of Academic Writing)

Here you might, for example, write the entire brief like you are telling a story—the story becomes the phenomenon and intentionality helps you tell it. Another possibility is that you write this as a theoretical (thought) piece in which you put other philosophical thinking outside of phenomenology in dialogue with intentionality.

One reason I like to use this assignment is that it requires us to turn ourselves over to the philosophical concept of intentionality and tie it to something concrete and meaningful to our lives. Of course, this parallels the phenomenological project writ large. Another, related reason I like the assignment is that we end up getting to see all sorts of creative and insightful readings of intentionality. I close this chapter with a phenomenological encounter containing excerpts from Dr. Joseph Pate's phenomenology brief.

Phenomenological Encounter #3
Excerpts from a Phenomenology Brief

My family and I once lived in an old farmhouse, originally built in the late 1800s. The kitchen window looked out on a 40-foot tall split-trunked sweet gum tree. Behind the tree was a large water tower, over 200 feet high, standing erect and imposing like some sentinel or large sundial. The window faced south, and suctioned to it was a gift given to my daughter: a small crystal ball attached to a solar panel that operated a tiny motor which, when hit by the sun's rays, would animate the ball, turning it in a circular motion. The rays would pass through the crystal sending dancing prismatic rainbow splashes circling around the kitchen. My newborn daughter and I would watch, mesmerized, as we were gifted with a light show of passing beauty. Due to the location of the tree, tower, clouds, and our sporadic presence, the light show, when it occurred, was novel, rich, full. It was within this experience that a grander understanding revealed itself. Accentuated by the lyrics of the Grateful Dead song *Scarlet Begonias*—"Once in a while you get shown the light in the strangest places if you look at it right" and those dancing prismatic rainbows, I find myself understanding something of intentionality.

What is it to find myself understanding *intentionality*? It is a collective gathering of life experiences and relations, both passive and active.... In reading Husserl, Heidegger, Van Manen or Dahlberg, I experienced definitions of intentionality. They are captured in quotes, phrases, and glossaries, all discursive tools to provide me (subject) with the experience (object) of intentionality as defined.... Intentionality understood and experienced lacks formational and relational understanding. The definitional process is finalized, complete, and resolved.

When I read, think about, and conceptualize these definitions, I *experience* each of them. I may even venture to say that I *know* what intentionality is, because I am able to memorize the definitions, or capture them for a publication, a test, or a conversation. These definitions demarcate parameters and boundaries. Additionally, through these definitions, not only do I *know* what intentionality is, but I simultaneously *know* what it is not. For example, it is not reincarnation, or sustainability, or revolution. I even may define intentionality to mean the act of coming in contact with the world, living in the world, and through the reflective process, making meaning of the world. *What* is lacking, however, is meaning-making and an active understanding of intentionality. . . . .

Levinas offers this perspective of intentionality:

> Intentionality is thus an intention of the soul, a spontaneity, a *willing*, and the sense bestowed itself, in some way, what is *willed*; the way in which beings or their Being manifest themselves to thought in knowledge corresponds to the way in which consciousness "wills" this manifestation through its own resolve or through the intention that animates this knowledge. (Levinas 2002, 530)

Departing from previous definitional attempts of intentionality, Levinas elevates the soul. The soul is used to show the present, active engagement in the world opposed to the mind which retrospectively understood the world.... Intentionality transcends any reduced, cookbook recipe that forces me to relegate relations with the world to mere experience. Intentionality requires my participation by rejecting my defining.

CHAPTER THREE

The Importance of Prepositions

One might wonder: why devote an entire chapter to prepositions when nouns, verbs, adjectives, and adverbs are most often considered to be the key players in writing—those parts of speech out front and noticeable?

It is because the prepositions operate as the connective tissue—the flesh as Merleau-Ponty would say—that allow meanings to slip, slide, turn, dissolve, emerge, explode, die, come to life. And I believe it is in prepositions that our growing understandings of phenomenological philosophies can be operationalized in our crafting of phenomenological research. So, the reason this content is placed here is that I think it can allow us to make a successful transition from philosophy to methodology without losing philosophical potency in our methodology, and yet begin to give us some concrete mechanisms to guide us.

In this chapter I argue that to begin to understand phenomenological philosophies and their implications for phenomenological methodologies it is important to dig into "of," "in," and "through." As I stated in the section introduction, I will continue to work across a number of philosophers and philosophical ideas. For the sake of clarity here, I have decided to line up each preposition with a particular phenomenological approach: "of" with the Husserlian, "in" with the Heideggerian, and "through" with my post-intentional approach. I actually don't think the distinctions are nearly as sharp as I have suggested here,[1] but I have found time and time again that blurring these lines too early in our craft, before we even know there are lines at all, can lead to confusion, and sometimes to frustration.

I also want to note that I have purposefully been more succinct in this chapter for two reasons. First, I want this chapter to help us dwell a bit more on philosophy and then draw the philosophy to a close. Second, I do not want us to get too deep into methodology until Section 2. I begin with "of."

The Importance of the Preposition "Of" in Early, Husserlian Phenomenology

As has been touched upon before, Husserl—in his phenomenology—had set out to put back together what Descartes had severed centuries earlier. For Husserl there was no way for subjects to be separated from the world (referred to as "objects" in philosophical parlance). That is, the subject (the individual "I", ego, self) was always connected meaningfully with everything else in the world. At first brush this seems like yet another statement of the obvious. However, Husserl's philosophical move here turned centuries of Western philosophy on its head, since Descartes had argued that the subject was contained, in and of itself so to speak, in meaning.

I would argue that the most important word in Husserl's proclamation that consciousness is always "of" something is, in fact, the word "of", as "of" then becomes the transitory word that connects the subject with objects. Staying with this logic, when one is crafting phenomenological research following Husserlian phenomenology one is studying the "of-ness" of a phenomenon. One is not studying the subjective lived experiences of those who have experienced the phenomenon. Again, early phenomenology assumes that consciousness is not contained in individual subjects, but out in the intentional relations between subjects and the world. The word "of" also signifies to Husserlian phenomenologists that meaning belongs to the intentional relation between subject and object. One is not studying the subject or the object, but a particular intentional relationship (i.e., of-ness) between subject and object.

As I have debated phenomenology with qualitative researchers who do not practice phenomenological research, this has been one point of contention. The central sticking point involves the determination of where meaning belongs. In other qualitative research methodologies, those that focus on studying the experiences of others such as narrative research, self-study, and ethnomethodology, the individual experiencer is treated as the meaning-maker and in ethnography the meanings are seen as cultural manifestations. I have found it challenging to clearly describe how phenomenology differs from this point of view, as the distinctions are subtle yet discernable. In order to help make sense of these matters here, I offer another list of key points to consider.

1. When one is studying intentional relations following Husserl, one must have an experiencer—the subject in philosophy—and something that is experienced—the object in philosophy. However, one is not studying the subject or the object exclusively. One is studying the relationship between the two, a relationship that might be love, hate, concern, struggle, understanding, learning, dying, communicating, disagreeing, forgiving, resenting, and so on. The latter represent phenomena, that is, intentional relations between subject and objects. They are a few of the innumerable intentionalities that may exist. These are the foci, the units of analysis, for phenomenologists.

2. Related, we might conceive an "of" intentional relationship as illustrated in Figure 3.1. The subject and the object are connected through a one-way arrow, and the circle signifies that when we study a phenomenon we need to carefully tend to the subject, the object,

Figure 3.1

and the intentional relation connecting the subject and object. That is, we need to focus on the intentional relation as it is lived between subject and object. In a colloquium led by Swedish phenomenologist Karin Dahlberg (summer 2005) she emphasized that some have even suggested that all that exists philosophically and methodologically speaking is intentionality (the arrow in the image above), and therefore, as a phenomenological researcher we must always stay focused on studying the particular intentional relation and not the subject and the objects of their intending. I go almost this far when I describe the importance of the preposition "through" in this chapter, and when I describe post-intentional phenomenology in section 3. However, when emphasizing Husserlian phenomenology and the importance of the preposition *of* here we will stay with the image shown in Figure 3.1 and say that there must be a subject and an object (e.g., a person in love with another person) in order for there to be an intentional relation in the first place.

3. The final point I want to make here concerns the direction of the intentionality in Husserlian phenomenology. I read Husserl's point that consciousness is always *of* something as still placing the genesis of the consciousness with the subject, which is then *directed* to the object of the intending. So, while Husserl did something incredibly important for Western philosophy, his conception did continue to situate the relationship such that it proceeds from the individual (subject, ego, "I") out toward the world. This will become important as we move to the prepositions "in" and "through."

The Importance of the Preposition "In" in Hermeneutic, Heideggerian Phenomenology

This time we begin with the image and then unpack how conceiving of the phenomenon and the intentional relation as "in" differs from "of" (see Figure 3.2). Heidegger is often credited with bringing phenomenology and hermeneutics together. In our recent article, Freeman and I (Freeman and Vagle 2013) suggest that, since Heidegger, phenomenology and

Figure 3.2

hermeneutics have had a grafted relationship, thus making the two (post-Husserl) difficult to distinguish. This is important to know as you make decisions regarding your craft.

I think it is possible to craft a phenomenological study that does not explicitly involve hermeneutics. However, I think one would be deciding to almost exclusively follow Husserl's early phenomenology, because when one decides to follow Heidegger, one is now entering into the grafted relationship between hermeneutics and phenomenology.

So, what does this mean for your craft?

To address this question, I turn to my recent article with Melissa Freeman (Freeman and Vagle 2013) and draw from some key arguments we make there.

1. The grafted relationship between hermeneutics and phenomenology, via Heidegger and then extended in Gadamer, places *being* at the center of philosophy and the social sciences. This is significant, as now the question becomes less about consciousness, and more about what it is to be in the world in various intentional ways. Phenomenological questions, following this line of thinking, move away from epistemological (to know) concerns, to ontological (to be) concerns. Phenomena, in this case, are conceived as the ways in which we find-ourselves-in the world—in-love, in-pain, in-hate, in-distress, in-confusion.

2. To take this a step further, Freeman and I stress that the grafted relationship between hermeneutics and phenomenology "was a radical ontological fusion of language and being. Heidegger was not only critical of phenomenology's (and philosophy's) instrumental use of language but was most critical of the way language was positioned as secondary to the phenomenological project. For Heidegger, language is not only the manifestation of a thing: it is the thing itself." (Grondin 2003, 727)

This second point can help us begin to see significant distinctions between the philosophical assumptions that undergird Husserlian and Heideggerian phenomenological research approaches. To review, in Husserlian phenomenology the intended meanings are conceived in a human's consciousness, which is always "of" (directed toward) something. Given this assumption, when one crafts Husserlian phenomenological research one is studying the directed of-ness of intended meanings.

In Heideggerian phenomenological research, intended meanings are conceived in being and language, which are always, I would argue, found "in" intersubjective relations. In this way, phenomena are not directed from subjects out into the world. They come into being and in language as humans relate with things and one another, again, "in" the world. Given this assumption, when one crafts Hedeggerian phenomenological research one is studying the *in-ness* of intended meanings. Returning to this image, the arrows leading back and forth between subjects and objects signify an intersubjective relationship. The subject is not conceived here as directing

Figure 3.2

the meaning. Rather, the intended meanings come into being. Humans *find-themselves-in* states of being. Again, crafting phenomenological research consistent with these philosophical assumptions would mean that the craftsperson become comfortable with putting the word *in* in front of the phenomenon.

When sharing this particular point in courses and lectures, participants and I have found ourselves aware that adding the word *in* seems comfortable in some cases and not as comfortable in others, particularly in American English—mostly, we have theorized, because the phrasing is more or less present in everyday conversation. For instance, it seems to work well in cases such as *in-love, in-pain, in-distress, in-despair, in-recovery*—but less so in cases such as *in-hate, in-resistance, in-learning, in-understanding.* Regardless, of how "normal or abnormal" it feels to utter a phenomenon with *in* in front of it, if you find-yourself-drawn-to an *in-ness* approach to phenomenological research I strongly encourage you to become comfortable doing so. It can help us learn to also become more comfortable seeing our craft as an ontological project.

Turning ourselves over to this becomes even more important if we become drawn to a *through-ness* approach.

The Importance of the Preposition "Through"

Over the years, phenomenological researchers have disagreed—sometimes sharply—as to whether one is or should be seeking to describe or interpret phenomena through the phenomenological research act (Dahlberg 2006; Giorgi 1997; Vagle 2009). Given my situating of "of-ness" and "in-ness" in this chapter, this might not come as much of a surprise. This disagreement has its origins in Husserlian and Heideggerian philosophies and has been fueled, over time, by those who have continued to practice these two main philosophies, and the respective descriptive and interpretive phenomenological research approaches stemming from these philosophies. Having studied and practiced both approaches I have found myself oscillating between embracing the distinction between the two pimary approaches and strongly resisting the need to make a hard and fast choice between them. I have tried to write my way through my early struggles to make such a choice (Vagle 2009). What I found in writing that piece is that although I understand the desire to find some middle ground between the two approaches (Dahlberg; Finlay 2008a), I have become much more interested in trying to re-imagine the matter outside of a descriptive-interpretive dualism. My re-imaging has taken various twists and turns over the past few years, influenced by conversations with those outside phenomenology who think debating such a dualism is a big waste of intellectual and practical time and energy, as well as by conversations with those inside phenomenology who stand in relation to this dualism in unique and powerful ways.

Although I aim to offer another possible approach for those interested in working in the phenomenological tradition, I am by no means the first to tinker and play with other possibilities. As I will describe in a bit more detail in Section 2, Linda Finlay (2008b) has moved beyond a two-pronged dualism by mapping out what she refers to as "variants of phenomenology." My purpose here, as we close our consideration of philosophical foundations for phenomenological research, is to emphasize that we stand in an age of philosophical and methodological proliferation of approaches to phenomenology. Although you might decide to focus your craft on early phenomenology—whether it be Husserlian or Heideggerian—there are all sorts of other possibilities. And I would argue that these various possibilities—especially my post-intentional approach—are not philosophically conceived as "of-ness" or "in-ness," but as "through-ness." To explain, I begin with an image introduced in Chapter 2 (see Figure 3.4).

Because we are limited here to a two-dimensional, static medium, I cannot make this image do for me what I need it to, so I will use words to expand on what you can see in Figure 3.4. I imagine the lines of this image being permeable and malleable: they are not rigid, nor are they finite. Like intentional meanings, they shift and change in and over time, through ever

Figure 3.4

changing contexts. The lines of overlap and grey areas signify some salient, partial, fleeting, temporary, unstable intentional meanings. In this sense, the "of-ness" and "in-ness" of intended meanings are at best glimpses of possibilities. This is one reason why the preposition "through" works better. Here are three more reasons:

1. The preposition "through" signifies movement. Although phenomenological research grounded in a "through-ness" conception is still an ontologic project, it moves from a focus on being to a focus on becoming. Intended meanings are always in the process of becoming.
2. Related, if a "through-ness" image conceives intended meanings as always in the process of becoming, it also signifies that intended meanings are generative. That is, something becomes of the intended meanings in the process of their living out.
3. This then allows us to see intentionality as intentionalities, i.e., as multiple, partial, fleeting meanings that circulate, generate, undo, and remake themselves. In a "through-ness" conception there is not a linear link between subjects and objects. Rather, there are intentionalities of different shape, sizes, and contours running all over place.

If you choose to craft "through-ness" phenomenological research, you are chasing intentionalities and their various possibilities as they take complicated shape in multiple, sometimes competing contexts. Crafting this type of phenomenological research means that we embrace phenomena as social and not as belonging to the individual. Although consciousness does not dissolve in this conception, it is no longer a useful construct. I am not saying that humans are not aware or conscious of their experiences of phenomena (i.e., things do still manifest and appear, as discussed earlier). Rather, continuing to use the term consciousness in a "through-ness" conception would thrust us back, philosophically speaking, into the ego and would fail to embrace post-structual philosophies from, for example, Deleuze and Guatarri that have furthered what early phenomenology started to do: move away from the egocentric predicament that Sokolowski (2000) describes.

We do, of course, gather data from and interact with individual research particpants in a "through-ness" approach. However, when we go to individuals we acknoweldge that each individual is part of many larger social strata that have histories and traditions (as Gadamer 1975 proposes). These individuals are not "experiencing the phenomena" in isolation or in a vaccum. Their experiences are "shot through" the world. This also means that phenomena can be studied as they circulate through objects—films, depictions, art, poetry, pictures. In other words, direct accounts are not the only way phenomena circulate through intentional relations.

Another way to think about this is to imagine that we are entering into and moving through a "dialogue with" the phenomenon we are studying (Adams 2012). This dialogue is both literal and figurative. It is literal in that we may craft phenomenological research designs that explicitly involve dialogues with others about their experiences of the phenomenon. It is figurative in that our interpretations, growing understandings, theorizing, and debating are dialogic, that is, they are moving and shifting through the questions we pose, observations we make, and assertions we proffer. In Section 3, I will spend time expanding upon this philosophical notion and its implications for methodological matters.

Resource Dig (Section 1)
Phenomenological Philosophies

The purpose of each resource dig is to provide you with a relatively small and targeted group of resources that I anticipate will be helpful as you hone your craft. My use of the term "dig" here is to signal that our crafting will involve some wading through and mucking about various ideas, thoughts, insights, interpretations, and conceptions of what phenomenological researchers try to do. I find it incredibly important to avoid a narrow view of the craft, and instead simply trust that as crafts-women and -men we will make the decisions we need to in order to create something beautiful (to us at the very least!) with our creations. The list here is not exhaustive by any means. I made choices based on my experiences with these texts. I include additional resources at the end of the book. So, here are some important and useful philosophically-oriented resources that I and others often turn to for guidance, inspiration, and assistance. Happy digging!

Websites

http://www.phenomenologyonline.com/
http://www.maxvanmanen.com/

Although there are all sorts of useful phenomenology websites, I have found these two sites managed by Max van Manen to be the deepest and richest resources for philosophical and methodological guidance. The resources cover a lot of philosophical ground, especially phenomenologyonline.com, and then, of course, they dig deeply into how van Manen conceives of phenomenology.

Texts

I have grouped the texts based on how I tend to use them in my crafting and teaching of phenomenological research. I list the selected texts first and then describe why I have found them most useful.

Introductions to Phenomenological Philosophies

Moran, D. 2000. *Introduction to phenomenology.* Routledge: New York.
Moran, D., and T. Mooney, (Eds.). 2002. *The phenomenology reader.* New York: Routledge.

I have found these two texts useful in simultaneously highlighting salient philosophical ideas, deeply considering these ideas, contextualizing the phenomenological movement in continental philosophy, and introducing key phenomenological philosophers. I routinely refer to them for guidance and assistance.

Sokolowski, R. 2000. *Introduction to phenomenology.* New York: Cambridge University Press.

I have used this text to introduce newcomers to phenomenological philosophy. Sokolowski explicitly tells the reader that he is not going to "cite" in the traditional academic sense, and instead sets out to carefully unpack and describe important philosophical ideas in phenomenology. I have found his work pretty accessible for folks new to the philosophy. However, as I have discussed throughout this section of the book, it is important to turn ourselves over to the complexities of these philosophies, to allow ourselves the space to not immediately understand, and instead to revisit these ideas over and over again.

Another set of resources that I do not list in full here (see *Additional Resources* section), but do want to mention is Continuum's *Guide for the Perplexed* series. There is a *Guide for the Perplexed* book for nearly all major phenomenological and post-structural philosophers. These texts are written by present-day philosophers who are scholars specializing in Husserl or Heidegger or Gadamer, etc.. They tend to write pedagogically about their respective philosopher's work and are able to emphasize important concepts and draw out nuances and changes to the philosopher's writing and thinking over time. I highly recommend this series.

Dahlberg, K. 2006. The essence of essences—The search for meaning structures in phenomenological analysis of lifeworld phenomena. *International journal of qualitative studies on health and well-being* 1:11–19.
Freeman, M. and Mark D. Vagle. 2013. Grafting the intentional relation of hermeneutics and phenomenology in linguisticality. *Qualitative Inquiry* 19(9):725–735.

Although different in purpose than the books just described, these two articles are examples of how specific philosophical ideas can be continually re-interpreted and re-cast for new purposes, and in doing so, help deepen one's understanding of the original philosophical ideas.

Original Sources

Considering what I have said so far, it is incredibly important to also go to the original sources themselves, especially if you find yourself wanting to situate your crafting deeply in any one philosopher's work. Here are some original works that I like to use.

Deleuze, G. and Felix Guattari. 1987. *A thousand plateaus: Capitalism and schizophrenia.* Minneapolis, MN: University of Minnesota Press.

Gadamer, H-G. 1975. *Truth and method.* New York: Continuum.

Foucault, M. 1994. *The order of things: An archaeology of the human sciences.* New York: Vintage Books.

Heiddegger, M. 1998 [1927]. *Being and time,* trans. J. Macquarrie & E. Robinson. Oxford: Blackwells.

Husserl, E. 1970 [1936]. *The crisis of European sciences and transcendental phenomenology,* trans. D. Carr. Evanston, IL: Northwestern University Press.

Merleau-Ponty, M. 1995 [1945] *Phenomenology of perception,* trans. C. Smith. London: Routledge Classics.

Sartre, J-P. 1943. *Being and nothingness: A phenomenological essay on ontology,* trans. H. E. Barnes. New York: Washington Square Press.

Schutz, A. 1967. *The phenomenology of the social world,* trans. G. Walsh and F. Lehnert. Evanston, IL: Northwestern University Press.

SECTION TWO

Phenomenological
Research Approaches

In this section of the book we will consider the following questions:

1. What are some of the possible approaches to conducting phenom-enological research? **(Chapter 4)**
2. What are some of the key methodological strategies and tools one can use when crafting phenomenological research? **(Chapters 5 & 6)**

Throughout section 1, I referred to the craft of conducting phenomenologi-cal research as both approach and methodology. The latter is the more com-mon term used, in social science research writ large, to describe the particular ways in which systematic inquiry is carried out. However, I have seen the former term—approach—used regularly by some high-amplitude phenom-enologists. This choice of language is not happenstance and is based, I think, on an active resistance, following Gadamer, to method becoming rigid and coveted, as though the method itself is the thing that brings about the "truth" of matters. For instance, Dahlberg, Dahlberg, and Nystrom (2008) write:

> To be a methodological servant means to avoid research restrictions and a rigid, lockstep use of method. Openness ... means to have the patience to wait for the phenomenon to reveal its own complexity rather than imposing an external structure on it, such as the dogmatic use of theories or models. (p. 112)

Although my "writing for clarity" instinct tells me to just pick one or the other and be consistent, I decided instead to foreground *approach* in this section and then use *methodology* as well. Why?

1. To me, the word "approach" signals something concrete *and* something open, malleable, flexible, and agile. The word does not feel fixed. Max van Manen (2001) likes to return to the etymological roots of im-portant words and terms to help the reader understand the idea on a deeper, more meaningful level. In one such case, van Manen traces the word "method" back to its origins, "methodos," which translates as the phrase "a way." Following a way (a path, an approach) to do something allows us, as phenomenological craftspeople, to have parameters, tools, techniques and guidance, but also allows us to be creative, exploratory, artistic and generative with our craft.
2. Alternatively, the term "method," as enacted in research methodologies, can often be read as linear and step-by-step. Although this is not necessar-ily the case, I do want to strongly encourage an open approach to crafting phenomenological research. Gadamer, in *Truth and Method* (1975), helps us understand the importance of openness and questioning, and I think it is important to bring this attitude to our research design work.

With this "approach to approaches" in mind, throughout this section I provide methodological options, and although my preference is obviously for the post-intentional approach I have developed, in this section I focus on a few other approaches. Making decisions about what to emphasize was difficult, as there are numerous approaches and how they are named is nuanced. My decision, though, was to briefly address some of the presumably lesser known approaches and then settle in with the most recognizable. I begin in chapter 4 working through what Linda Finlay (2008b) describes as "variants of phenomenology," in order to clearly lay out possibilities. I go into greater depth with descriptive and interpretive phenomenological approaches, as they have well-established histories in the social sciences and are still the most commonly practiced approaches. I decided to frame chapters 5 and 6 around consistent methodological questions I have received when teaching, presenting, mentoring, discussing, and debating phenomenological research. Throughout both chapters, I articulate methodological tools and strategies in response to these questions, all of which, I think, can be useful to some degree in any phenomenological research approach. Given the range and depth I have sought, this section is the longest of the book. As in section 1, I close section 2 with a *resource dig*—this time focusing specifically on methodological matters.

CHAPTER FOUR

Possible
Methodological Approaches

There are many methodological approaches available for phenomenological researchers. In this chapter I spend some time describing various approaches to crafting phenomenological research. Before I begin, it is important to distinguish methodology from research methods.

> Research methodology has many dimensions and research methods do constitute a part of the research methodology. The scope of research methodology is wider than that of research methods. Thus, when we talk of research methodology we not only talk of the research methods but also consider the logic behind the methods we use in the context of our research study and explain why we are using a particular method or technique and why we are not using others so that research results are capable of being evaluated either by the researcher himself or by others. Why a research study has been undertaken, how the research problem has been defined, what data have been collected, what particular method has been adopted, why a particular technique of analyzing data has been used, and a host of similar other questions are usually answered when we talk of research methodology concerning a research problem or study. (Para. 1, http://blog. reseapro.com/2012/05/research-methods-vs-research-methodology/, retrieved August 3, 2013, Reseapro)

In this chapter, I focus on research methodology—the broader scope of the research design, logic, assumptions, etc. And although I will mention a thing or two about particular research methods, namely data gathering and analysis tools and strategies, as parts of broader research methodologies here, I devote chapters 5 and 6 to a more substantive consideration of tool and strategy.

I begin with an excerpt from a helpul piece Linda Finlay has written. Finlay (2008b) emphasizes the two primary and longstanding approaches that I have been discussing thus far—descriptive and interpretive phenomenology—and then proceeds to offer up more possibilities, some of which she characterizes as types of hermeneutic approaches: heuristic, lifeworld, interpretive phenomenological analysis (IPA), critical narrative, and relational. I offer Finlay's variants, directly, here as a way to frame the range of available possibilities.

Phenomenological Encounter #4
Finlay's Articulation of Variants

(Note: This is taken directly from Finlay [2008b, 2]).

The information indented below illustrates something of the variations in approach by showing how research questions, focus and methods vary subtly. For example, if six phenomenologists, each utilising a different method, were researching the experience of "feeling lost," they might phrase their research question along the following lines:

A *descriptive empirical phenomenologist* might well ask: "What is the lived experience of feeling lost?" They might compare the protocols (written descriptions) offered by participants about one instance of feeling lost and attempt to identify the essential or general structures underlying the phenomenon of feeling lost.

The *heuristic researcher* could well focus more intensely on the question: "What is my experience of feeling lost?" While they might draw on a range of data from stories, poems, artwork, literature, journals, they would also look inward, attending to their own feelings/experiences by using a reflective diary. They would aim to produce a composite description and creative synthesis of the experience.

A *lifeworld researcher* would ask "What is the lifeworld of one who feels lost?" Collecting and analysing interview data, they would focus on existential themes such as the person's sense of self-identity and embodied relations with others when experiencing a feeling of being lost.

The *IPA researcher* would focus on "What is the individual experience of feeling lost?" They would aim to capture individual variations between co-researchers. Thematic analysis would involve some explicit interpretation on the part of both co-researcher and researcher.

The *Critical Narrative Approach researcher* would ask "What story or stories does a person tell of their experience of feeling lost?" having interviewed perhaps just one person. The analysis would be focused on the narrative produced and how it was co-created in the research context.

The *Relational researcher* might similarly interview just one person asking "What is it like to feel lost?" They might focus on the co-researchers' self-identity and "creative adjustment" (their sense of self, their being-in-the-world and the defensive way they've learned to cope). The research data would be seen to be co-created in the dialogical research encounter and the relational dynamics between researcher and co-researchers would be reflexively explored.

Where to Start?

Given the continual growing, shifting ways in which phenomenological research is practiced, those new to crafting phenomenological research are often left with questions about where to start. As I stated in the introduction, phenomenology is not a singular concept, idea, or methodology. And even though phenomenolog(ies) stem from a set of similar philosophical commitments and understandings, phenomenological methodologists understand, interpret, and apply the philosophy differently.

Some may lament the fact that there is not a single, crystal clear, and unified way to craft phenomenological research. However, for me, this lack of singularity, certainty, and finitude is the beauty of crafting phenomenological research. One gets to enter into a moving and shifting dialogue with these methodologies. I do not perceive this as ambiguous in a negative sense, but rather, as an opportunity to explore and play with ideas, phenomena, and ways of inquiring about ideas and phenomena. I think as we hone our craft, being versatile (i.e., turning with ease from one thing to another) is an important goal. All of this said, the phenomenological craftsperson has to have a place to start and needs to have a way to proceed.

Throughout the remainder of this chapter, I point to some possible starting points and ways. Again, instead of saying relatively little about many possibilities, I chose to say a bit more about three possibilities: Giorgi's (2009) modified Husserlian approach to descriptive phenomenology; van Manen's (2001) hermeneutic (pedagogical) phenomenology; and Dahlberg, Dahlberg, and Nystrom's (2008) reflective lifeworld approach. By no means do I do any of them justice. Each of these high-amplitude phenomenologists have written entire books explicating their respective approaches. My goal here is to simply point you to their unique ways. Please go to them directly if their perspectives speak to you. And as I have mentioned, I devote the entire 3rd section of this book to the "post-intentional phenomenological research approach"—my unique perspective and way of crafting phenomenological research.[1]

Giorgi's (2009) Descriptive Phenomenology— A Modified Husserlian Approach

Since, for Husserl, phenomenology was never less than a philosophy, the method he articulated was a philosophical one and so I will present his version of the method first even though I will add modifications to it in order to have it serve scientific purposes. (Giorgi 2009, 87)

This seemingly simple statement is quite important if you choose to craft phenomenological research using or drawing heavily on Giorgi's approach. Giorgi is careful not to directly equate Husserl's philosophical method with the descriptive phenomenological method he proposes. However, he does in my opinion stay as close to Husserl as any high-amplitude phenomenologist I have read. When modifying Husserl's philosophical method to meet the expectations and demands of conducting human science research, Giorgi emphasizes the importance of going to the descriptions of others; assuming the attitude of the phenomenological reduction (bracketing); and the search for an invariant psychological meaning—all of which are important to consider briefly here.

Getting the Descriptions of Others

Giorgi consistently uses the word "description" to communicate both the data one collects from those who have experienced the phenomenon and what the researcher crafts (i.e., a description) in order to communicate the invariant meanings based on his or her analysis. When getting the descriptions of others, Giorgi emphasizes interviews and also includes drawing on the writing of experiences. He distinguishes between the researcher's and the research participant's role in the process, the latter being responsible for describing the experience from the natural attitude, that is, the everyday, taken-for-granted way we tend to move through the lifeworld, and to provide a description "that is as faithful as possible to the lived through" (p. 96). The researcher's role is to take this raw data and analyze it from "within the phenomenological reduction" (p. 96).

Assuming the Attitude of the Phenomenological Reduction

Giorgi stresses the importance (necessity, even) of employing the phenomenological reduction in order to describe the phenomenon. Although others have distanced themselves from the reduction (e.g., Dahlberg, 2006; Finlay, 2008a; Vagle, 2009), Giorgi goes so far as to say that "no claim that an analysis is phenomenological can be made with the assumption of the attitude of the phenomenological reduction" (p. 98). Given Giorgi's strong feelings in this regard, I advise those choosing to craft phenomenological research using his approach to spend considerable time learning about the phenomenological reduction, which is referred to as "bracketing" as well. Although I discuss bracketing at some length in chapter 5, it is important to address it here in relation to Giorgi's approach. The origins of the phenomenological reduction stem from Husserl, and involve different levels, the most radical being the transcendental reduction in which "one transcends the perspective of human consciousness" (p. 98). Giorgi retreats from asking phenomenological researchers following his approach to achieve this level of reduction, and instead advocates for the psychological phenomenological reduction.

> With this reduction, the objects of experience are reduced (that is, reduced to phenomena as presented), but the acts of consciousness correlated with such objects belong to a human mode of consciousness. (p. 98)

This distinction is important to understand as descriptive phenomenological research approaches are often directly and literally equated to Husserl's concept of transcendentalism. Clearly, transcending one's consciousness in order to study the consciousness of others is a tall order. In Giorgi's approach one is asked to use human consciousness to study human consciousness and is asked to bracket his or her past understandings and knowledge in order to be able to analyze the raw data from a fresh perspective.

Search for an Invariant Psychological Meaning

Another distinguishing feature of Giorgi's approach is the search for invariant structures of meaning. It also represents what I think is Giorgi's most significant modification of Husserlian phenomenology. In Giorgi's earlier work (e.g., 1985, 1997), he spoke of finding the essence of the phenomenon as an important pursuit for those practicing phenomenology. In his most recent work, work that we are now considering, he distances himself a bit from essence, much like other high-amplitude phenomenologists.

> So, instead of searching for essences through the method of free imaginative variation, I seek the structure of the concrete experiences being analyzed through the determination of higher-level eidetic invariant meanings that belong to that structure. (p. 100)

There is much from this excerpt that must be learned in order to craft phenomenological research following Giorgi's approach. As I have stated previously, it is important to go directly to the source to begin to understand the complexities. Here, though, I think it important to understand that Giorgi has moved away from pursuit of a universal essence, even though Husserl called for it in his philosophy. Even an ardent follower of Husserl now acknowledges the difficulty of translating the idea of a philosophical essence to human science research. It is also important, though, to note that Giorgi still advocates for a highly-structured analysis process that pursues eidetic (i.e, the shape of a thing) invariant (i.e., that which does not change or vary through contingencies and contexts) meanings that are part of a structure. So, if you choose to follow or draw heavily upon Giorgi's modified Husserlian approach, you are not pursuing a universal essence but you are searching for invariant meanings that belong to a structure.

Steps of the Method

Although the purpose of this chapter is to lay out broader methodological commitments and not dig too deeply into the details of data collection or gathering and analysis until chapters 5 and 6, given the structured nature of Giorgi's approach I do go into some detail here. I go into less detail when discussing van Manen and Dahlberg et al.'s approach in this chapter because I interpet their approaches as being less structured and more open and malleable.

In order to search for invariant meanings, Giorgi articulates a concrete process for data collection and analysis.

1. Data collection phase: Although Giorgi acknowledges that written descriptions can yield phenomenological data, he spends the vast majority of his time explicating the primacy and importance of interviews. Here I want to stress that although Giorgi favors the unstructured nature of phenomenological interviewing, his analysis is quite structured—this, of course, makes sense given that in his approach the goal is to search for invariant meanings that belong to a structure. Given the structured tone his analysis procedure takes, keep in mind that Giorgi is absolute in his belief that "everything that is collected has to be analyzed. (Phenomenology's holistic perspective demands that all of the data that are collected be analyzed)" (p. 124). He cautions the researcher, then, to be sure to not have interviews run too long.

2. Analysis of descriptions: I have chosen to include a somewhat lengthy excerpt from Giorgi, because I think it clearly points to one important indicator of his commitment to descriptive phenomenology.

   > A descriptive analysis, however, in principle, does not try to go beyond the given. The point to be established now is that a descriptive analysis attempts to understand the meaning of the description based solely upon what is presented in the data. It does not try to resolve ambiguities unless there is direct evidence for the resolution in the description itself. Otherwise, one simply tries to describe the ambiguity such as it presents itself. Thus, the attitude of description is one that only responds to what can be accounted for in the description itself. The descriptive researcher obviously sees the same ambiguities that an interpretive analyst would see but is not motivated to clarify them by bringing in nongiven or speculative factors. (p. 127)

   Although, as you will see in Section 3, I see these matters quite differently, if you agree with Giorgi in this regard make sure you situate your data collection and analysis with this view of descriptive analysis in mind. It would mean, I think, that if you follow this approach it is wise to become skilled at not only noticing when you see ambiguities in the descriptions, but also resist the urge to interpret those ambiguities, both of which point back to Giorgi's call for the psychological phenomenological reduction in the form of bracketing.

3. Concrete steps of Giorgi's descprive analysis method: Like most high-amplitude phenomenologists, Giorgi advocates a commitment to whole-part-whole analysis. For Giorgi, this first involves reading for a sense of the whole. This most often means that one reads the entire interview transcript to get a sense of the entire description. Then Giorgi suggests that the researcher moves to identification of

parts—what he terms "meaning units." Do not set up an a priori (be-forehand) criteria to determine meaning units, and do not question the meaning units. Rather, as you carefully re-read, make note of each time you perceive what Giorgi refers to as a "shift in meaning." Finally, you are to transform "participant's natural attitude expressions into phenomenologically psychologically sensitive expressions" (p. 130). This is the process by which the structure and invariant meanings are articulated.

Max van Manen's Hermeneutic (Pedagogical) Approach

To do hermeneutic phenomenology is to attempt to accomplish the impossible: to construct a full interpretive description of some aspect of the lifeworld, and yet to remain aware that lived life is always more complex than any explication of meaning can reveal. (van Manen 2001, 18)

As I articulated in the introduction, my first encounter with phenomenology was through my interactions with van Manen just over a decade ago. It is important to note that van Manen (2014) has written a new book, *Phenomenology of Practice: Meaning-Giving Methods in Phenomenological Research and Writing.* Like mine, it is published by Left Coast Press and was released about the same time as this text. Although it is not possible for me to discuss van Manen's most recent thinking given that both of our books were being crafted simultaneously, if you are drawn to his approach I strongly encourage you to go to his new book and his earlier work for guidance.

When I return to van Manen's (2001) text, *Researching Lived Experience: Human Science for an Action Sensitive Pedagogy,* I feel as though I am return-ing to my phenomenological home. This particular quote has this quality for me, as it reminds me that if we craft phenomenological research following van Manen our work is something we actively do; is an interpretive act; and is something that is never final. If you choose to follow van Manen's approach, I think these three methodological commitments are central.

In addition, van Manen stresses how hermeneutic phenomenology is the study of lived experience; explication of phenomena as they pres-ent themselves to consciousness; the study of essences; the description of experiential meaning we live as we live them; the attentive practice of thoughtfulness; a search for what it means to be human; and a poeticizing activity (pp. 8-13). Although there is not space here to adequately address each of van Manen's important points here, it is important to get a sense of van Manen's perspectives on crafting phenomenological research. When I read van Manen's phenomenological work, I can feel his commitments to thoughtfulness, pedagogy, and poetics. And perhaps this particular quote best captures how van Manen would like us to "approach" his approach.

In the works of the great phenomenologists, thoughtfulness is described as a minding, heeding, a caring attunement (Heidegger 1988 [1927])—a heedful, mindful wondering about the project of life, of living, of what it means to live a life. (p. 12)

Philosophically speaking, I interpret van Manen's appoach as "in-ness" phenomenological research. It is one methodological way to open up how we find-ourselves-in the world. The approach strikes a wondering, contemplative tone that resists finality and rigidity. There is an open quality to how phenomena are explored and described. When describing salient points of his approach, I often say that van Manen writes "poetically about how to write poetically." And although I encourage anyone interested in his approach to by all means proceed, I also suggest that if you are drawn to structure, steps, and frames, that using his approach might be challenging. He is quite serious in his resistance to a priori steps and structures in the name of precision, exactness, and rigor, as he believes that devising a methodology to accomplish these attrtibutes can stifle the very fabric of doing human science research in a hermenuetic phenomenological tradition.

> Rigorous scientific research is often seen to be methodologically hard-nosed, strict, and uncompromised by "subjective" and qualitative distinctions. "Hard data" refers to knowledge that is captured best in quantitative units or observable measures. In contrast, human science research is rigorous when it is "strong" or "hard" in a moral and spirited sense. A strong and rigorous human science text distinguishes itself by its courage and resolve to stand up for the uniqueness and significance of the notion to which it has dedicated itself.... This means also that a rigorous human science is prepared to be "soft," "soulful," "subtle," and "sensitive" in its effort to bring the range of meanings of life's phenomena to our reflective awareness. (van Manen 2001, 17–18)

I have always been drawn to the open, malleable, responsive ways that van Manen describes and practices his approach to phenomenology. I find it inviting, hopeful, and consistent with underlying assumptions of "in-ness" hermeneutic, interpretive phenomenologies in that it seems to reflect the ever-shifting nature of the lifeworld and the interpretive flow of how humans move in the lifeworld. So, given the ever-changing, shifting nature of his approach, how does van Manen suggest that we craft a methodological way to proceed?

He offers six research activities that are in dynamic interplay with one another:

1. *Turning to a phenomenon that seriously interests us and commits us to the world.*

   For van Manen, this involves identifying a phenomenon that we can deeply and thoughtfully settle into and sit with. He describes this process of turning to a phenomenon as a "being-given-over to some quest, a true task, a deep questioning of something that restores an original sense of what it means to be a thinker, a researcher, a theorist." (p. 31)

From a practical standpoint, regardless of the approach you choose, identifying your phenomenon of interest takes time, care, and reflection. Given van Manen's strong commitment to contemplation, wondering, and questioning, I think it is even more important to slow down and think deeply about the phenomenon. What do you REALLY care about? What potential phenomena do you actually want to learn more about?

2. *Investigating experience as we live it rather than as we conceptualize it.*

For van Manen, the distinction between "living" experience and "conceptualizing" experience is not subtle, and is, therefore, very important to understand when following his approach. Here van Manen is explicitly staying true to Husserl's call for phenomenologists, and actually all social scientists, to turn "to the things themselves." As previously discussed, the things are phenomena, and van Manen's primary point with this research activity is that when we conduct phenomenological research our methodological decisions should always help us draw out the concrete ways in which phenomena are lived and not how they are represented, conceptualized, or abstracted.

Practically speaking, it is important to ask yourself questions such as: What is it like to experience this phenomenon? What are all the possible facets and aspects of this phenomenon? We do not want research participants to unpack the phenomenon, connecting to other phenomena, etc. Rather, we want research participants to bring us to their experiences of the phenomenon. In chapters 5 and 6 I write in explicit terms about how to select research participants and gather data from participants. For now, it is important to keep in mind that to craft phenomenological research following van Manen's approach and perspective, it is critical to understand the difference between how phenomena are lived day-to-day, moment-to-moment in the natural attitude and how phenomena are conceptualized through representations, models, frameworks, and so on based on how they are lived.

3. *Reflecting on the essential themes which characterize the phenomenon.*

Van Manen writes: "phenomenological research consists of reflectively bringing into nearness that which tends to be obscure, that which tends to evade the intelligibility of our natural attitude of everyday life" (p. 32).

Said in a different way, phenomenologists love to study the things we tend to assume we know—the things we think we have settled.

One characteristic of the natural attitude is that we are in-action. Our acting, moving, speaking, decision-making, and so on are "simply happening." This, of course, makes sense and is necessary in order to live a life. The obscureness van Manen speaks of is that we simply do not notice the underlying phenomenological meanings as we live them. What we are reminded of in van Manen's approach is that when we craft phenomenological research, we are trying to cull meanings of things we do not typically see as we are moving in the lifeworld.

One day, not long ago, a doctoral student came to me wondering whether his study was phenomenological. After a crash course of sorts in some of what I have articulated in this book, we discussed the core purpose of the research. He was interested in what motivated a particular group of students who routinely seemed unmotivated and unmotivat(able). I responded by asking the question: What do we take motivation to be? This question led us down a long, winding road that ended with the realization that he did not care to study what it was to live "in-motivation" or "in-unmotivation." He wanted to study that which might provide motivation. The interesting and important question for phenomenologists is to open up that which we assume we know—in this case, motivation. A phenomenological question would focus on what it is to be motivated or unmotivated.

4. *Describing the phenomenon through the art of writing and rewriting.*

I am pretty confident that it was my early interactions with van Manen and his work that led me to approach the work of data gathering and analysis as a text that is to be crafted. I will describe some tools and strategies in chapter 6. For now, it is important to emphasize that as one moves through van Manen's methodology, activities 3–6 become intricately intertwined as you write your way to themes, and the writing and thematizing is deeply imbued in the intricacies of language, "of questioningly letting that which is being talked about be seen" (p. 33). Here we see the deep hermeneutic roots of van Manen's approach.

It is hermeneutic in that he is interested in opening up the lingusiticalities (Gadamer 1975) of the intentional relation. This "in-ness" approach reflects the grafted relation of linguisticality (language) and intentionality. For van Manen, there is no way to pry language and meaning apart, and hence no way to do phenomenology without it being an analysis of language. This also means that if you choose to follow van Manen's approach, you cannot escape the interpretive nature of the work. Although van Manen calls for bracketing and the phenomenological reduction, he is not suggesting that one becomes a describer of meaning. One is not bracketing interpretations, but is bracketing pre-suppositions as one interprets.

5. *Maintaining a strong and oriented pedagogical relation to the phenomenon.*
Van Manen's concern with this activity is that the researcher stays deeply committed to the phenomenon under investigation—that your early interest in the phenomenon remains throughout the study. This requires a deep and thoughtful engagement through data gathering, analysis, writing, re-writing, and so on. For van Manen, this has a pedagogical quality, one in which you become and remain situated as teacher-learner in relation to the phenomenon. He wants us to actively want and need to learn as much as possible about the phenomenon, and through our writing, wants us to communicate the essential themes in such a way that others learn from the text and hopefully have phenomenological nods along the way.

6. *Balancing the research context by considering parts and whole.*
In order to not get lost in the never-ending maze of language, van Manen, like most high-amplitude phenomenologists, emphasizes the importance of thinking about one's phenomenological description through parts and wholes. This idea has deep philosophical roots and has both methodological and technical qualities. The utilization of a parts and whole process for van Manen, unlike Giorgi, is not about identifying invariant structures (of-ness) of the phenomenon. To be sure, van Manen does discuss essences, but not in the final, structured sense Husserl philosophized. Rather, van Manen, as he articulates in research activity 3, is interested in the essential themes and these themes come to be for the researcher as he or she steps "back and look(s) at the total, at the contextual givens, and how each of the parts needs to contribute toward the total" (pp. 33–34).

In *Researching Lived Experience,* van Manen devotes a chapter to each of these research activities, all of which would be important to read and re-read if you want to draw on all, most, or even some of van Manen's perspectives.

Dahlberg, Dahlberg, and Nystrom's (2008) Reflective Lifeworld Research Approach

Rather than formal steps or protocols, the necessary approach for lifeworld research is characterized by an aspiration for sensitive openness, a concern for elucidation, and a purposeful leaving aside of expectations and assumptions so that the phenomenon and its meaning can show itself and, perhaps, surprise its researchers. (Dahlberg, Dahlberg, and Nystrom 2008, 96)

In their book, *Reflective Lifeworld Research,* Dahlberg, Dahlberg, and Nystrom's commitment to openness is clear and consistent, as is their resistance to method in a step-by-step manner. This means that we must take on an open attitude when identifying the phenomenon, choosing participants, gathering data, analyzing data, and when presenting results. For Dahlberg et al., openness is important because it involves becoming aware of how the phenomenon reveals and conceals itself to the researcher and demands that the researcher pay attention to how she or he influences and is influenced by the phenomenon.

These three facets of openness permeate all other methodological considerations in Dahlberg et al.'s approach, the most notable being the move away from, in my opinion, the phenomenological reduction and bracketing to the concept of bridling. I discuss the move in some detail in chapter 5, but it is also important to illimunate it here as well, given its primacy to Dahlberg et al.'s approach.

In phenomenology circles, Dahlberg's (2006) and then Dahlberg et al.'s (2008) departure from a more strict application of Husserl's phenomenological reduction and bracketing is no small thing. I recall sitting in a colloquium, led by Dahlberg toward the end of my doctoral studies (Summer 2005), when Dahlberg was in the midst of making this move. She shared with us that she came to the point in her work as a phenomenologist—what I would call the "honing of her craft"—where she realized that although she had been stating that she bracketed her pre-understandings, assumptions, and so on, in reality she was doing something different.

> Neither researchers nor anyone else can cut off one's pre-understanding, that little vexation that constantly has occupied philosophers as well as researchers, but it can be "bridled" from having an uncontrolled effect on the understanding. (p. 128)

When I reflect on my ongoing growth as a phenomenological craftsperson, I cannot stress enough Dahlberg's influence on my enacting of phenomenological philosophies and methodologies. Just as welcoming and "at home" I felt and feel with van Manen's phenomenology, so I do with Dahlberg's, and although they have similar commitments, their approaches do differ. They both are most certainly interested in being open and responsive to the phenomenon, but Dahlberg, Dahlberg, and Nystrom's (2008) reflective lifeworld approach works across hermeneutics and phenomenology, actually making it difficult (and undesirable) to categorize it as interpretive or descriptive. I assume this is one of their goals—not wanting to reify a descriptive-interpretive dualism, and instead to work across these two traditions.

However, using my "of-ness, in-ness, and through-ness" heuristic, I would characterize their approach as primarily an "in-ness" approach. The ontological nature of the methodology is quite strong, as they are most concerned with how the phenomenon is revealed through the research act. This is perhaps why they highlight three factors we should consider when

choosing what and how we will gather data: "the nature of the phenomenon; the research question in its context; and the aim to go to the things
themselves, i.e., to practice a 'bridled attitude' to the phenomenon of study
and the research process" (p. 176).

1. *The Nature of the Phenomenon.*

The more complex and ambiguous a phenomenon seems to be,
the more it requires sensitive choices of data gathering methods....
Sometimes a phenomenon needs to be approached by one method
initially, and later, other means and methods can be chosen. Methodological creativity and ... a multiplicity of methodological means in
research are important (p. 176–77).

As is clear in this excerpt, Dahlberg et al. continue to advocate for
openness. Remaining open to how the phenomenon calls to be studied
means approaching the entire research process in a contemplative,
philosophical way. I have sensed this in Dahlberg from the moment I
met her and began to spend time with her work. I think Dahlberg et
al.'s point here is incredibly important. In order to craft phenomenological research it is important to slow down and really dwell with the
phenomenon. I know how difficult this is. There are deadlines around
every corner and constant demands on our time. However, if we can
"schedule time to slow down" we can then approach our craft with the
immediacy and presence necessary to really see what phenomenon we
want to study and how that phenomenon wants to be studied.

2. *The Research Question in its Context.*

It perhaps could go without saying that the research question is
important to this and any research approach. However, Dahlberg
et al. want to be sure that those practicing their reflective lifeworld
research understand that the research question is not being devised
in a vaccum—they want us to explicitly tie the research question to
context. I find this to be a unique feature of their approach, and one I
amplify in my post-intentional approach. If we decide to craft reflective
lifeworld research we need to explicitly situate the phenomenon, the
research question, and the data gathering strategies in context. This
means that the context matters—that when we describe or interpret
the phenomenon, the description/interpretation will be contextualized.
The contextual aspects that surround those living the phenomenon
will need to be illuminated and explored.

3. *The Bridled Attitude.*

As will be further described in chapter 5, it is a bridled attitude—the
commitment to openness throughout the entire research process—
that is central to Dahlberg et al.'s approach. Given the importance of
achieving and maintaining this attitude, I think it is important to take

a bit more time with this aspect of their approach. Dahlberg et al. suggest that in reflective lifeworld research, it is difficult to determine in advance all steps in one's method..In fact, they feel that sometimes the only thing that can be planned in advance is the overarching research question, and that the open and bridled attitude and the sensitivity for the phenomenon and its context is the first consideration—not the "method."

Moving toward openness—the phenomenological attitude as Husserl imagined it, the bridled attitude as Dahlberg et al. imagine it—has proven difficult for some as they begin to learn the craft of phenomenology. This is one moment in which I encourage a turn to visual and performing arts for guidance. My daughter is active in musical theater, and as such I have found myself involved in theater in ways that I had not been earlier in my life, sometimes building sets, other times playing a bit role when they need an adult in a children's production. What has struck me is how phenomenological the entire theater process feels to me. I have even suggested that some of the best phenomenologists—in their living in the world and their practice— are artists. I think the commitment to openness and performance are present in musical theater, as well as in the careful crafting of film.

On occasion, when I teach phenomenology I use films to help us make some sense of the openness this type of research requires. As I discussed in the book's introduction, I am drawn to the film *Peaceful Warrior* (Salva and Bernhardt 2006) as I think it provides important insights and openings for openness.

So, in reflective lifeworld research the choices for data gathering are nearly limitless. However, Dahlberg et al. do not hold the same perspective when it comes to carrying out data analysis. In fact, this is the only place where I find them to explicitly depart from their strong commitment to openness, stressing that their unlimited approach is not applicable to communicating research findings.

Dahlberg et al. lay out both descriptive and interpretive analysis processes that reflect the typical ways in which these analyses are carried out—that is, their descriptive approach aligns fairly closely with Giorgi's process described above and their interpretive approach reflects the interpretive, textual analysis present in van Manen's approach. One notable difference, though, between Giorgi's and Dahlberg et al.'s analysis processes is that Dahlberg et al. continue to use the concept of essence, whereas Giorgi has modified his approach to focus on invariant meanings within a structure. My sense is that this might be a semantics issue, but I also think it is important for those interested in one of these approaches to pay attention to these sorts of details. Finally, I think, like Giorgi and van Manen, there is a strong commitment to some variation of a whole-parts-whole analysis in Dahlberg's descriptive and interpretive analysis procedures.

The Commitment to Methodological Coherence

What I have emphasized in this chapter is merely a taste of the possible approaches for the phenomenological craftsperson. The goal was to provide you with a place to start and a sense of the commitments some high-amplitude phenomenologists make as they have honed their craft. Although there are clear differences among the approaches I chose to discuss, sometimes in philosophy, sometimes in practice, and other times in semantics, there are a number of similarities as well. For instance, all three see the whole-part-whole analysis process as necessary. All three continually return to specific aspects of phenomenological philosophy to provide the basis for their unique approach to phenomenological research. For Giorgi, this is most often to Husserl; for van Manen, to Heidegger and Gadamer; and for Dahlberg, et al., to Merleau-Ponty and Gadamer.

Today, I think the phenomenological craftsperson is working at an exciting time. We have many options available to us. I think it is possible to choose a particular approach, study it deeply, and then follow that approach closely. I think it is equally possible to choose aspects of various approaches and combine them in unique ways. Regardless of which path we choose to take, I think it important to be able 1) to clearly lay out the commitments our methodologies hold, 2) to advocate for the choices we make and defend them philosophically and methodologically, especially if we choose aspects of various approaches; and then 3) to articulate the philosophical and methodological coherence as we craft.

We now turn our attention to practical tools and strategies for crafting phenomenological research.

CHAPTER FIVE

Tools and Strategies for Crafting Phenomenological Research

I decided to frame this chapter and chapter 6 around consistent questions I have received when teaching, presenting, mentoring, discussing, and debating phenomenological research. The questions in this chapter that I address range from how to identify a phenomenon of interest to how to address issues of researcher reflexivity and validity in phenomenological research. In chapter 6, I address questions regarding data gathering and analysis. In both chapters, I do not organize my responses to the questions by research approach. Instead, I discuss how, if at all, I think the question should be addressed differently depending on approach. Otherwise, it is safe to assume that I think the question can be addressed basically in the same way across phenomenological research approaches.

I also have made a concerted effort to provide concrete examples. It is important to note that in this chapter I spend less time weighing in on the tools and strategies and more time putting a variety of tools and strategies out for your consideration. This means that I move fairly swiftly, with the idea that you can/will choose to go directly to the sources I cite if a particular tool or strategy speaks to you. I will, however, slow down a bit in section 3 when discussing how some of these tools and strategies take unique shape in my post-intentional research approach.

How do Phenomenological Researchers Tend to Concerns for Validity?

It is perhaps not customary to begin a chapter such as this with issues regarding validity. However, the way that I see validity being pursued in phenomenological research influences other consideration of methods. So, I begin with validity.

Dialogues Regarding Validity in Qualitative Research

Although a substantive analysis of how validity has been discussed in qualitative research is beyond the scope of this book, it is important to note that validity has been weighing on the minds of qualitative researchers for many years, that there is no single way in which validity is imagined and enacted in qualitative research, and that phenomenological research is framed, to some degree, by these broader conversations regarding validity in qualitative research.

Freeman and colleagues (2007) described validity in qualitative research over the last three decades in an effort to demonstrate the various, sometimes competing ways in which qualitative researchers have treated validity when conducting studies and to resist a single hegemonic definition of validity in qualitative research. To these ends, Freeman and colleagues highlight various terms used in parallel with validity, such as trustworthiness, credibility, relevance, and confirmability, to name a few. They also note that validity has been discussed in general (e.g., Kvale 1995; Lincoln 1995; Miles and Huberman 1984), within specific traditions such as ethnography (e.g., LeCompte and Goetz 1982), self-study (e.g., Feldman 2003), and post-modern, feminist, critical, and post-structural designs (Lather 2001; Scheurich 1993). Freeman and colleagues stress that validity has been and continues to be a debated and contested ground and that future discourse regarding validity should preserve this heterogeneity instead of attempting to squelch it in the name of establishing standards of quality.

As a phenomenological craftsperson, I have found entry into discussions of validity to be marked primarily by a consideration of the researcher's sustained engagement with the phenomenon and the participants who have experienced the phenomenon. This sustained engagement has been described as requiring the researcher to be open and sensitive to the phenomenon under investigation (e.g., Dahlberg, Drew [Dahlberg in 2008], and Nystrom 2001, 2008; van Manen 2001) throughout all phases of the study. From a technical standpoint, phenomenological researchers have tended to use the technique of bracketing, which, again, stems from Husserl's philosophical notion of the phenomenological reduction. And as we considered briefly in chapter 4, Dahlberg (2006), followed by Dahlberg, Dahlberg, and Nystrom (2008), have forwarded bridling as an alternative to bracketing. We go deeper with these notions here, as they relate to validity.

Although it can be debated whether bridling is simply a subtle name change for the bracketing process, I argue that bridling is a significant departure, methodologically and philosophically, from bracketing and can be read as more fully reflecting Scheurich's (1997) call for new imaginaries of validity and contributing to what Ritchie and Rigano (2001) describe as a dialogue "that might highlight multiplicity and differences rather than reinforce the regulatory dualism that divides the privileged Same (as in conventional scientific practices) from the as yet untheorized Other" (2001, 753).

Moving from Bracketing to Bridling in Phenomenological Research

Giorgi (1997) stresses that the phenomenological reduction demands that the researcher bracket "past knowledge about the phenomenon encountered, in order to be fully present to it as it is in the concrete situation in which one is encountering it" (p. 240). For Giorgi, the task of bracketing does not mean removing all past knowledge. Rather, it involves putting aside or rendering non-influential this knowledge. Giorgi is particularly concerned that past interpretations will determine the study of present phenomena and thus will not adhere to rigorous research standards. In keeping with his concern for rigor, Giorgi asserts that when properly executed, the phenomenological reduction preserves what is presented in the natural attitude except that it moves beyond stating something "is" and states that something presents itself as actually existing. What makes the phenomenological reduction significant, then, is that it allows for the very examination of why one comes to say something "is." Giorgi (1997) even stresses that, "No work can be consider (sic) to be phenomenological if some sense of the reduction is not articulated and utilized" (p. 240).

To me, Dahlberg's (2006) move to bridling is significant and is a result of her contemplative reflection about what it means to "live" as a phenomenological researcher as she is doing phenomenological research:

> Inspired by the philosophies of Husserl and Merleau-Ponty, and not least by Giorgi's interpretation of them, I early saw the importance of the phenomenological reduction. However, the term "reduction" was not a hit, too loaded with philosophical implications, and for a long time I worked hard to find a better term for research. Marked by my existence on a horse ranch I then found the term "bridling." (p. 16)

Dahlberg's move to bridling refers to her lived experience on her horse ranch, earlier research involving bridling (e.g., Carlsson et al. 2004) and epistemological work related to bridling (Dahlberg & Dahlberg 2003). For Dahlberg (2006), bridling accomplishes two primary things. First, bridling involves the essence of bracketing in that pre-understandings are restrained so they do not limit the openness. Second, bridling is an active project in which one continually tends to the understanding of the phenomenon as a whole throughout the study. Dahlberg, Dahlberg, and Nystrom (2008) add that bridling is forward-looking and that bracketing looks backwards, focusing on preunderstandings and trying to limit their influence on the present.

Considering Dahlberg's second point more fully, to bridle one's understanding of the phenomenon she suggests that we take on a reflective, open stance. We bridle understanding so that we do not understand too quickly or carelessly or that we do not attempt to make definite what is indefinite (Dahlberg & Dahlberg 2003).

Bridling means a reflective stance that helps us "slacken" the firm intentional threads that tie us to the world (Merleau-Ponty 1995). We do not want to cut them off and we cannot even cut them off as long as we live, but we must, as Merleau-Ponty encourages us to, loose (sic) them up in order to give us that elbow room that we need to see what is happening when we understand phenomena and their meanings. (Dahlberg 2006, 16)

For Dahlberg (2006), this elbow room means gaining some distance from the phenomenon so that the researcher might see the phenomenon in a different way. This amounts to taking on a phenomenological attitude as opposed to a natural attitude (Dahlberg and Dahlberg 2003), again where we do our everyday living. In the natural attitude we do not reflect as we are living—we just live. However, when we take on a phenomenological attitude in phenomenological research we are bridling. We are "'actively waiting' for the phenomenon, and its meaning(s), to show itself" (Dahlberg 2006, 16). Actively waiting for the phenomenon combines the ideas of seeking and remaining open to receive. It means being patient and attentive when exploring the relationship, as Dahlberg (2006) states, between the subject and the phenomenon and then also between the researchers and the subjects in the intersubjective relationship. In this way, bridling is a reflexive act.

How do Phenomenological Researchers Practice Researcher Reflexivity?

Researchers across fields (e.g., Macbeth 2001; Alvesson, Hardy, and Harley 2008) have spent considerable time describing how we might strive to be reflexive in our research. Focusing on research in the field of organization and management theory, Alvesson, Hardy, and Harley discuss four sets of textual practices researchers have used—multiperspective, multivoicing, positioning, and destabilizing. Although Alvesson, Hardy, and Harley see all four practices as worthwhile, they point to the inherent limitations of each. For example, although multiperspective textual practices aim to keep the researcher from producing a grand narrative, Alvesson, Hardy, and Harley wonder how researchers can implement all perspectives equally when they most certainly have their own preference.

In the field of education, Macbeth (2001) has raised similar concerns with regard to what he describes as two of the three expressions of reflexivity—positional and textual. As a result, Macbeth offers a third expression—constitutive. When considering Macbeth's analysis of reflexivity in education, there are glimpses of bridling in all three expressions of reflexivity he describes but cannot say that bridling can or should be exclusively seen in any one of them. Although Macbeth's intent is to critique and perhaps disrupt both the positional and textual reflexivities and offer the constitutive reflexivity found in ethnomethodology as a useful alternative, his argument can be used to locate bridling in all three expressions.

68

For instance, Macbeth (2001), much like Alvesson, Hardy, and Harley (2008), describes positional reflexivity as how the researcher positions himself or herself in the world and articulates his or her commitments to interrogate such positioning. This interrogation is intended to notice what might remain unnoticed throughout the research process, namely those positions that perpetuate hegemonic relations. To this end, positionally reflexive research acknowledges the primacy of the researcher in the research act.

Bridling in phenomenological research sets out to accomplish much the same result. When bridling, we try to cull our agency so that our agency alone does not determine the phenomenon. Bridling, then, can be seen as a meaningful way to be skeptical (Freeman et al. 2007) of what we "know" when conducting phenomenological research. At the same time, it is important to recognize that this skepticism harkens back, as Macbeth stresses, to similar concerns during the Enlightenment—that through disciplined inquiry one could see the world in ways beyond ordinary experience. When crafting phenomenological research it is important then to become skeptical of our seeing, but it is equally important to be mindful of phenomenology's interest in understanding the meaning of lived experience. In this respect, the ordinary lived experience is the very thing the phenomenological crafts-person should aim to explore and not something to aim to move beyond.

At the same time, it is necessary to recognize that when we aim to understand lived experience more fully, we are crafting written expressions of these experiences. Therefore, our bridling is also present in what Macbeth (2001) calls textual reflexivity. Again, like Alvesson, Hardy, and Harley (2008), Macbeth draws on some of Woolgar's (1988) thoughts on this matter. Macbeth (2001) stresses that reflexively textual practices involve "the reflexive monitoring of the text in its production" (p. 43). Although this monitoring might take many forms, Macbeth spends considerable time discussing Lather and Smithies' (1997) use of north and south to divide their text. The northern hemisphere contains the edited narratives of the participants' voices, whereas the southern hemisphere contains the authors' reflexive voices as they articulate their positionality and interests. The reader, then, is able to see both the rich narratives and the reflexive thoughts in one textual space. This textual practice is important, as is the caution Macbeth (2001) offers: "There are endless texts—instructions, directions, or writings on the blackboard—whose sense and organization are inseparable from the occasions of their production and use. Rather than objects for contemplation, these texts are first and routinely objects embedded in the practical achievements of common understanding" (p. 47).

To Macbeth (2001), constitutive reflexivity is not a methodological move, nor is it a representational language game. Instead, it turns away from analytic endeavors and toward that which is constituted in the actions of the participants. "This is an order of reflexive work that attaches to the everyday worlds and to the competent practitioners who produce and sustain them. We could usefully say that they are the first reflexive analysts on the scene" (p. 54).

Macbeth's (2001) point here resonates, for going to the everyday worlds of those who experience a given phenomenon—the thing as intended(Dahlberg 2006)—is a core purpose of phenomenology. However, the things to which phenomenologists refer are not necessarily the observable actions of participants. Rather, they are the intentional meanings that make a phenomenon that particular phenomenon. When we craft phenomenological research we are interested in accessing those intentional meanings. Nevertheless, like the ethnomethodologist, we must understand that the intentional meanings are not really the result of the analyst's reflexive work but are always already there in the experiences of those who have experienced the phenomenon.

That said, I do not think it is fair to state that bridling is only a constitutive reflexivity, nor is it solely positional or textual. As Alvesson, Hardy, and Harley (2008) assert, it seems smarter to combine various reflexive practices in order to minimize the limitations each holds. To this end, bridling[1] can be imagined to some degree as all three, in that reflexivity is always already present in the phenomenon regardless of whether or not we are looking and is equally always already present in everything we do methodologically—beginning with the identification of the phenomenon of interest.

How do I Identify a Phenomenon to Study?

The practice of bracketing (if you choose to go with descriptive phenomenology), or bridling (which is what I would use with the other approaches mentioned thus far) begins the moment you begin to consider the phenomenon you want to study. And as stressed in chapter 4, you will find that identifying your phenomenon of interest is substantively addressed whatever approach you take to crafting phenomenological research. Although it might seem as though this would be one of the easier tasks, I have found the opposite to be the case. Why?

First, sometimes researchers new to phenomenology assume the phenomenon is the same as the research problem or topic. As I articulated in section 1, a phenomenon in phenomenology means something much more. Phenomena manifest and appear in our living in and through the lifeworld. In my discussion of "of-ness", "in-ness", and "through-ness", I even suggested that we put the preposition "in" in front of various states of being in order to get a deep, felt sense of a "phenomenon" (e.g., in-love, in-pain, in-recovery). But even in this play with language, how do we come to find a phenomenon?

In order to begin to identify a meaningful phenomenon to study, be sure to get oriented to the phenomenon. I have had researchers new to this work state that this seems somewhat awkward and abstract—get oriented, they ask? I think a good way to make this less awkward and more practical is to think about orienting yourself to the phenomenon as follows:

- Find a phenomenon for which you are passionate—some vexing problem people live with and through.
- Spend time with the phenomenon before doing any formal data collection—write, read, discuss, watch films, contemplate.
- Make every effort to not get too attached to your initial thoughts about the phenomenon under investigation. Although your initial thoughts might end up serving as "the" phenomenon when all is said and done, don't make this the expectation. Remaining open to what the phenomenon might become is important, especially early in this process.
- Once you feel you are getting closer to the phenomenon you want to study, be sure to question, wonder, and reflect as much as you can about what you think it is like to experience this phenomenon. This will not only help bring clarity to the phenomenon you want to study, but it will give you a good start practicing the openness phenomenological craftwork requires throughout the entire research process.
- From the start, remember that the phenomenon and the intentional meanings that run through and "make up" the phenomenon's very fabric is the unit of analysis (i.e., the "thing" that is being studied).

The key things to remember when identifying a phenomenon of interest is to slow down, wonder, contemplate, change, discuss, and pay attention to how you feel when you sit with the phenomenon a bit. Do not be afraid to ask others to think through this process with you. Sometimes we do not know what we think and feel about phenomena until we work through it with others.

How do I Handle the Literature Review in a Phenomenological Study?

It is to the researcher's advantage to be acquainted ... with published research reports and other types of literature. However ... it can even be advisable not to read too much ... existing literature on the very phenomenon. Knowing ... much about "how it is" can make it hard to "bridle" enough to enable the researcher to see something new. (Dahlberg, Dahlberg, and Nystrom 2008, 174)

The important point with regard to this particular question is: how much is "enough" when it comes to reviewing relevant literature, and then, from a phenomenological perspective, how much is too much?

In one sense, it seems silly to even consider this question, as research generally tends to include some sort of substantive acknowledgement of what previous research has informed/is informing what is to be studied. Sometimes the literature review serves as a funnel of sorts. One begins broadly and continues to narrow toward the focus of the inquiry. Other times the literature review is written more as an argument, where the researcher takes a more critical, evaluative stance in reviewing the literature. Whatever the case, I have found that the literature review is treated as a necessary step in the research process.

However, as can be seen in Dahlberg, Dahlberg, and Nystrom's point above, in phenomenological research there is a concern that reviewing literature might "sediment" (Buckley 1992) the phenomenon in research language and compromise our openness to what we might learn from the inquiry. I believe this concern harkens back to Husserl's early concern that the social sciences had fallen prey to the lure of positivism, and in doing so had moved too far away from studying the things themselves, phenomena. Phenomena, then, had become abstractions, representations, and theoretical models. This led Husserl and those who have followed to practice phenomenological approaches that actively resist such abstractions, representations, and theoretical modeling in favor of approaches that attempt to see phenomena as they are lived.

Returning to the question regarding the place for the literature review in phenomenological research, the concern is that existing literature would end up settling matters before the study was even conducted. So, although tracing existing literature seems to make good common research sense, in phenomenology it can put at risk the phenomenologist's philosophical and methodological commitment to remain as open as possible to the phenomenon. In my experience crafting phenomenological research, I have found the literature review helps me get clear about the phenomenon of interest and also to feel as though an exhaustive review of the literature is not time well spent, as it postpones the really important phenomenological work— opening up and exploring the phenomenon. As you will see in section 3, where I discuss post-intentional phenomenology, I advocate a partial review of the literature. I think the same might be useful with phenomenological research writ large for the following reasons:

1. It strikes some sort of balance between the customary research practice of conducting a literature review and not setting up an a priori explanation of what the phenomenon "is" or "should be" according to empirical explanations.
2. It read(ies) us for the phenomenon. That is, it orients us to the phenomenon a bit.
3. It helps us get more and more clear about the phenomenon we are studying.

I close this portion of the chapter with some basic considerations[2] to keep in mind when writing partial reviews of the literature.

**Phenomenological Encounter #5
The Partial Review of the Literature**

Interpretive Stance:
- The review attempts to provide a "big picture" of the major issues related to this area.
- Major issues are identified and explored descriptively and evaluatively.
- Connections across individual studies are made.
- Connections across the broader areas (clumps? sections?) are made.
- Instead of listing studies, the writer helps a reader develop a sense of how ideas and results relate to each other.
- The review should help establish the significance of the research.

Use of Evidence
- Generalizations are supported with clear examples and citations.
- The writer uses discretion about when and how much detail is needed.
- The review should be up-to-date.

Organizational Structure:
- Organization is clear and easy to follow.
- Headings and other devices (previewing, reviewing, etc.) are used as needed to help guide the reader through the paper, identify major points of the argument, and keep the focus clear.

What Role Does Theory Play in Phenomenology?

This question has been of some concern to me as I have crafted phenomenological research, and has been close to vexing for some of those I have mentored in their dissertation research—as scholars outside of phenomenology have, at times, taken issue with how phenomenology, especially old phenomenology, treats theory. For example, when I have suggested that using critical theory in a phenomenological study is fine as long as the researcher remains open to questioning what critical theory assumes and how it might influence how the phenomenon is approached, others have been perplexed. They have asserted that if critical theory is articulated as the study's theoretical framework, that it should then, indeed, frame the study. Given concerns such as this one, it is important to work through the role of theory in phenomenology.

Historically, theory has held a tenuous place in phenomenology. Husserl, in particular, envisioned a foundation for all of social sciences that resisted theory testing, theoretical explanations, and theoretical predictions. Although this almost seems antithetical to scholarly work writ large, it is important to step back and consider why Husserl was so adamant in this regard.

As I explain elsewhere in the book, positivism had served as the coin of the philosophical realm in Western thought for centuries, and as previously discussed (Sokolowski), one of the core tenets of positivism is that conscious-ness (understanding, meaning) resided in humans and was fully contained therein. It would follow, then, that when social scientists set out to do research, they took the lead of natural scientists. Social scientists created controlled experiments that set out to test theories, explain phenomena, and predict what might happen in given situations. The primary concern for Husserl was that such methods and philosophies actually moved researchers further and further away from the entire purpose of their investigation—to open up and learn more about what it is live in the world.

As has been discussed, those who follow Husserl's descriptive phenom-enology closely (e.g., Giorgi 1997, 2009; Moustakas 1994) have convinc-ingly argued that bracketing theories is a non-negotiable commitment in phenomenological research during data collection and early analysis. Yet, they ask researchers to bring important theoretical understandings from their scholarly fields (e.g., for Giorgi, psychology) to bear in later data analysis and when writing up findings. The argument, staying true to Husserl, is that theories—no matter how well constructed or agreed upon in a scholarly field—should not be used to determine or test the ways in which humans experience the world. Human experience is too complex, too fluid, and too ever-changing to be captured in, or worse yet, constrained by a theory. The point of "coming back to" the data using theories is to acknowledge that the work of a researcher is to contribute to ongoing theorizing. In sum, in Husserlian phenomenology, bracketing theories is an important part of early data collection and analysis, but using those same bracketed theories in later analysis to situate the work in particular fields is equally important.

In Heideggerian phenomenology, we take a decidedly different turn toward hermeneutics and the assumption that humans live in the world as interpretive beings in a continuously interpreted world. Furthermore, her-meneutic phenomenologists assume that it not only is impossible to avoid bringing theoretical assumptions to the work of qualitative research, but it is also undesirable to avoid theory. Interpretive phenomenologists such as van Manen have remained interested in the researcher bracketing his or her pre-assumptions and pre-understandings, but generally they feel as though it is important to bring all helpful texts to bear on one's interpretive understandings of the phenomenon under investigation.

In this way, theorizing becomes a central part of this approach to crafting phenomenological research. As I discuss in section 3 of this book, I have tried to re-conceive phenomenological research outside of a descriptive-interpre-tive dualism in favor of a post-intentional research approach (through-ness). A central commitment in my approach is to follow Dahlberg's move from bracketing to bridling (Dahlberg 2006; Vagle 2009) and now to what I am calling "post-reflexivity." I am particularly interested in how post-reflexivity can be practiced as a dogged questioning of one's knowledge as opposed to a suspension of this knowledge. In what I am imagining, theories are interrogated so they do not dominate or determine what is possible to see during data gathering and analysis, but this interrogation does not mean that theories are not always already running through data gathering and analysis. This apparent contradiction cannot be resolved, it can only be opened up. Thus the theoretical contradictions, to me, become interesting and important parts of the work because they are always already interesting and important parts of the lifeworld.

How Many Participants Should I Have in the Study and How Do I Choose Them?

Although this is, I think, an important question and consideration in any phenomenological research approach, regardless of which approach you choose to follow, it is important to heed Dahlberg, et al.'s advice regarding sample size. "The question of sample size is essential in research when using statistical calculation.... In lifeworld research the selection of informants is different.... One idea is that the more complex a phenomenon, the larger the group of informants." (p. 175)

I have not found there to necessarily be "magic numbers" of research participants. I encourage you to survey various phenomenological studies to see how researchers have handled this particular matter. I also encourage you to recite to yourself the adage that I have heard van Manen and Dahlberg utter, "the phenomenon calls for how it is to be studied." Practice openness as it has been discussed throughout this book. If it seems to make sense, relative to the phenomenon under investigation, to spend a lot of time with one or two participants in a particular context over an extended period of time and gathering data in many different ways, such as through interviews, observations, anecdotes, and performances, then have one or two participants. If it seems that spending relatively little time with ten to fifteen participants makes sense relative to the phenomenon under investigation, then have ten to fifteen participants.

In my first phenomenological study (2006), I studied what it is like for teachers to recognize and respond when students do not understand something in the "action-present" (i.e., on the fly) moments of their teaching. I was interested in the teacher's perceptions of these moments. I had eighteen participants. I either interviewed them once or asked them to write lived experience descriptions and then followed up with each of them via email to have them help me dig deeper into initial meanings that seemed salient to me during early analysis. In a study two doctoral students, Angela Coffee and Colleen Clements, and I are currently crafting we are exploring what it is like for teachers and their students to experience using photo-storying to create social class-sensitive elementary classrooms. We are interested in the photo-storying—where students and teachers take photographs of important aspects of their lives, interpret those photographs, and write with and from those photographs—as a phenomenon. We are spending time in two elementary school classrooms throughout a school year—collecting student work, interviewing teachers and students, analyzing photographs, and interacting via Google Hangout technologies. There are three teacher participants and as many as twenty-five student participants in each class-room. As one can see in these two studies, the phenomena are quite different and therefore, the number of participants, the type of data gathered, and the duration of the data gathering are all quite different.

Tying These Methodological Matters Together

Being able to clearly and cogently address the issues and questions articulated in this chapter is an important part of crafting phenomenological research. Having a strong understanding of concerns regarding validity, researcher reflexivity, reviews of the literature, the role of theory, identifying a phenomenon, and participant selection is necessary.

It is equally important to make sure that methodological matters considered in this chapter cohere with the aspects of phenomenological philosophy that speak to you. Just as the philosophical ideas you choose need to reflect how you see and move through the world, so must those that are methodological. Coherence must continue to be on the forefront of our minds as we make decisions regarding data gathering and analysis.

CHAPTER SIX

Data Gathering and Analysis in Crafting Phenomenological Research

As we now move explicitly into the strategic and technical aspects of crafting phenomenological research, the following cannot be overstated: the phenomenon and the accompanying research question is the most important consideration, and then all other questions of method follow. Often, when I serve on doctoral committees for students who are using a phenomenological approach, other faculty and sometimes students will ask questions such as: Is it ok to use observations in phenomenological studies? Do phenomenological studies involve fieldwork like ethnographic studies? Is it not true that all phenomenological studies must utilize the unstructured interview?

My standard response is "It depends." It depends on the phenomenon under investigation, the contexts in which it is being studied, how many research participants are involved, what fields of study you are trying to speak to—but most importantly, one needs to pay very careful attention and remain open, again, to the phenomenon. One must be willing to make a data-gathering and analysis plan and then, once carrying out that plan, be willing to make adjustments and explore new ways to open up the phenomenon. Of course, this has human subjects' approval implications, and although governed by federal policies, each local Institutional Review Board is nuanced in its application of these policies. My experiences at two institutions have been quite similar. If one finds it necessary to make changes in data gathering and analysis processes during the study, one should submit a change of protocol so that it can be properly reviewed and approved. I also encourage researchers to think broadly, from the start, about the possible data gathering techniques they might ask of human subject participants, and include these possibilities in their initial human subject applications. Finally, I have found that early, consistent, and thorough communication with your Institutional Review Board is necessary and very helpful.

Before proceeding, I want to say a word about my choice of the phrase "data gathering" rather than "data collection." Certainly the latter is the more commonly-used term in research, and I think it is just fine to use this term when crafting phenomenological research as well, especially when we are communicating to broader audiences. In other words, I would not make

Crafting Phenomenological Research, by Mark D. Vagle, 77–104. © 2014 Left Coast Press, Inc. All rights reserved.

this issue a "bottom line" for you. At the same time, I like the ontological nature of the word "gathering." It feels a bit more free, open, and inviting to me. It also makes me feel as though we could just as easily be taken up by the data than doing the taking.

> Subject-object and subject-subject relationships do not occur in a vacuum but in a world vibrating of meanings ... the responsibility ... is to ... find [one's] way through all these meaning relations and find the best means and the best use of these means in order to see the phenomenon. (Dahlberg, Dahlberg, and Nystrom 2008, 172)

I think this description of the lifeworld as being a world "vibrating of meanings" is incredibly important. When one studies a phenomenon, then, it can be said that one must find the best way to study vibrations. Vibrations are not static or clean or stationary. They are moving and dynamic. This is why, I think, it is critical to remain open to all sorts of possible ways to gather data, including what I describe here and what others such as Dahlberg, Giorgi, and van Manen describe in their texts. I also think it is important to go outside of phenomenological texts to see what data gathering tools and strategies might be of use.

What Sources of Data do Phenomenological Studies Typically Use?

Here I lay out a number of possibilities. Dahlberg, Dahlberg, and Nystrom reiterate their commitment to openness regarding data gathering, stressing that the researcher should feel free to use techniques "found in everyday life and in other research approaches" (p. 171), including standard techniques such as interviews, observations, and written descriptions, as well as artistic forms such as drawings and paintings.

I wholeheartedly agree with this statement and extend it in the following ways. I argue that an open mindset to data gathering is important and useful in all approaches to carrying out phenomenological research. I also argue that literally any source of data has the potential to help open a phenomenon of interest. I now discuss some data sources, beginning with the most often used—interviews, observations, and written anecdotes—and then continuing with some that perhaps are used a bit less often but are every bit as useful, with a particular emphasis on some arts-based methods.

Interviews

Although phenomenological researchers use a variety of interview strategies and techniques, the unstructured interview is the most popular for it tends to be the most dialogic, open, and conversational. It is important to remember that phenomenological research is not experimental, comparative, or correlational. It is not important to the phenomenologist how one interview is the same or different from another. Rather, all interviews are treated as exciting opportunities to potentially learn something important about the phenomenon. In many phenomenological studies it is not necessary, nor even desirable to ask the same questions in the same way. The goal is to find out as much as you can about the phenomenon from each particular participant.

Across many, if not all, approaches to phenomenological research this particular data-gathering technique allows us to practice the art of moving from the natural to the phenomenological attitude. I have found, though, that conversational interviews can be more difficult to enact than a structured and semi-structured protocol. For those who like structure, the open-ended nature of the unstructured interview can be intimidating. With this in mind, I offer some advice about how to get started.

1. I think it is a myth that the unstructured interview technique is "wide open" and without boundaries or parameters. To the contrary, this technique starts with a clear sense of the phenomenon under investigation and then the interviewer needs to be responsive to the participant and the phenomenon throughout. The structure or disciplined process comes into being throughout the interview—not through an a priori protocol. It is determined as one finds her or himself in the interview with a particular research participant. Max van Manen writes:

   > It is important to realize that the interview process needs to be disciplined by the fundamental question that prompted the need for the interview in the first place. Too often a beginning researcher enthusiastically goes about "interviewing subjects" using the so-called "unstructured or open-ended interview method" without first carefully considering what interest the interview is to serve.... Sometimes it happens that a researcher is confused about his or her real interest or research question, and then the interview is somehow expected to bring about that clarity. (Retrieved August 27, 2013 at http://www.phenomenologyonline.com/inquiry/methods-procedures/ empirical- methods/interviewing-experiences/)

   Van Manen goes on to warn that proceeding without a clear understanding of the phenomenon might result in interviews that become speculative and not necessarily focused on the concrete phenomenon under investigation. This leads me to my second piece of advice.

2. As stated earlier in this chapter, be sure to get oriented to the phenomenon, and when you get to the point of planning your interviews, re-orient yourself to the phenomenon. Spend time thinking, writing, discussing, drawing, walking, running, biking, swimming, singing and

dancing (I am not kidding) about it, and once you are working your way through your interviews, continue to re-orient yourself as you learn with and from your research participants.

3. I encourage you to think about interviews broadly—they might be one-on-one, in small groups, in large groups. In in-ness and through-ness research approaches they might be combined with observational methods. They might be planned and mapped out and they might be more impromptu. You might have planned three interviews with each participant, but during an observation you might notice something you want to talk to the participants about right away.

4. From an even more practical perspective, here are some interview tips:
   - Audio-tape the interview, and be sure to have a back-up. There are many digital audio recording devices, as well as software programs, that are very useful and reliable. I have used Olympus digital audio-recorders, *Garage Band* (a software program for the Macintosh oper-ating system), and most recently, a downloadable program *Audacity.*
   - Start small—a friend and colleague of mine at the University of Georgia, Amy Parks, likes to remind her students and colleagues that, when we do difficult and challenging work, something has to be small. I think this is good advice when thinking about interviewing. Manage your expectations of how the first interviews will transpire.
   - During the interview listen slowly, thoughtfully, and carefully. Remember that although this is a conversation, your role as crafts-person is to move into the phenomenological attitude—to look at what we usually look through (Sokolowski). The participants' role is to share her or his experience of the phenomenon as lived, in the natural attitude.
   - Take some notes, but not too many. I suggest this because I think if you start trying to script what is being shared you are less likely to obtain the openness and immediacy (Dahlberg, Dahlberg, and Nystrom 2008) necessary in this type of craftwork. I usually jot down words and phrases that strike me as important. During the interview, I do not analyze why these words and phrases seem important. I pay attention to my body—how it responds to these words and phrases. I then try to circle back to these words and phrases with my ques-tions as the conversation is flowing. Although some interviewers get very nervous about not taking more notes, remember that you are recording the interview—you will not lose what is uttered.
   - Let the participant talk—redirect her or him toward the phenom-enon when you find it necessary. Unlike Giorgi, I do not worry all that much about participants "getting off task." I err to the side of letting them talk and then taking the responsibility for regaining the focus on the phenomenon.

- Pay attention to moments in which you assume you know what something means, and then open it up through questioning. This is an incredibly important part of this data-gathering technique. Phenomenologists leave no stone unturned and like to study the very things that scholars, practitioners, and fields of study writ large think they (we) have figured out (made definite). Practice using questions to interrogate your own "definiteness." Consider using phrases such as, "tell me more about that," "I have an understanding of that phrase you just used, but can you tell me what it means to you?"
- Plan to conduct multiple interviews with each participant. Use your honest, humble appraisal of your first interviews to inform follow-up interviews. Remember, you are honing your craft.

I close my discussion of interviewing with a phenomenological encounter that I have used over the past few years when engaging those interested in learning about phenomenology. In 2011, former *Saturday Night Live* and *30 Rock* actor and comedian, Tina Fey, published a book entitled *Bossypants*. In one chapter, she describes some of her experiences learning the art and craft of improvisation. To make her point clear she includes a segment, *The Rules of Improvisation that Will Change Your Life and Reduce Belly Fat*, with the disclaimer, as a footnote of course, that improvisation does not actually reduce belly fat. I think these same rules, with some slight contextual adaptations, serve the phenomenological craftsperson well as we work to attain the open, wondering, curious, uncertain, and reflexive mind-set this work requires.

Phenomenological Encounter #6
Learning from Others with the Help of Tina Fey

(The following paraphrased excerpt, *The Rules of Improvisation that will Change your Life and Reduce Belly Fat,* is taken from pages 84 and 85 of Fey, T. [2011]. *Bossypants.* New York: Reagan Arthur Books/Little, Brown and Company—Hachette Book Group.)

The first rule of improvisation is **AGREE**. Always agree and **SAY YES**. When you're improvising, this means you are required to agree with whatever your partner has created. So if we're improvising and I say, "Freeze, I have a gun," and you say, "That's not a gun. It's your finger." ... our improvised scene has ground to a halt. But if I say, "Freeze, I have a gun!" and you say, "The gun I gave you for Christmas! You bastard!" then we have started a scene because we have AGREED that my finger is in fact a Christmas gun.

Now, obviously in real life you're not always going to agree with everything everyone says. But the Rule of Agreement reminds you to "respect

---

what your partner has created" and to at least start from an open-minded place. Start with a YES and see where that takes you . . .

The second rule of improvisation is not only to say yes, but **YES, AND.** You are supposed to agree and then add something of your own. If I start a scene with "I can't believe it's so hot in here," and you just say, "Yeah. . ." we're kind of at a stand-still. But if I say, "I can't believe it's so hot in here," and you say, "What did you expect? We're in hell." . . . now we're getting somewhere. . . . YES, AND means don't be afraid to contribute. It's your responsibility to contribute. Always make sure you're adding something to the discussion.

The next rule is **MAKE STATEMENTS**. This is a positive way of saying "Don't ask questions all the time." If we're in a scene and I say, "Who are you? Where are we? What are we doing here?" . . . I'm putting pressure on you to come up with all the answers.

In other words: Whatever the problem, be part of the solution. Don't just sit around raising questions and pointing out obstacles. We've all worked with that person. That person is a drag. . . . Speak in statements instead of apologetic questions. No one wants to go to a doctor who says, "I'm going to be your surgeon? I'm here to talk to you about your procedure? . . ." Make statements, with your actions and your voice.

Instead of saying, "Where are we?" make a statement like "Here we are in Spain, Dracula" may seem like a terrible start to a scene, but this leads us to the best rule:

THERE ARE NO MISTAKES, only opportunities. If I start a scene as what I think is very clearly a cop riding a bicycle, but you think I am a hamster in a hamster wheel, guess what? Now I'm a hamster in a hamster wheel. I'm not going to stop everything to explain that it was really supposed to be a bike. Who knows? Maybe I'll end up being a police hamster who's been put on "hamster wheel" duty because I'm "too much of a loose cannon" in the field. In improv there are no mistakes, only beautiful happy accidents.

As is clear by now, I am a huge Tina Fey fan. I find her work to be smart, thoughtful, and hilarious—a very fine combination that is hard to find. Beyond this though, I firmly believe that the four rules for improvisation Fey describes can not only change one's life but can also change the way we, as phenomenological craftswomen and men, engage in data gathering. I have included Fey's contributions here, not because the rules of improvisation only apply to interviewing, but because I think they can be particularly useful during all interview-type interactions.[1] In order to apply Fey's rules of improvisation to interview-type interactions, I first point out two differences between Fey's context and ours. First, when we are in a research relationship with participants our roles are different. You are learning about the phenomenon from the participant, and the participant is asked to share with you her or his experiences. In an improv sketch all participants basically have the same role—trying to build the improv sketch together. Second, and related, we are conducting research-based inquiry instead of trying to entertain an audience.

With these contextual differences in mind, let us consider the applicability of Fey's 4 rules of improvisation to interview-type interactions. I think these rules can be thought of as guiding principles or commitments toward achieving a mindset that can be used any time we are talking with an individual participant, small group, large group, or having more informal dialogues and discussions.

Rule #1: **AGREE**. *Always agree and* **SAY YES**

Of course, when we are interviewing others we will not necessarily agree with what they say, think, and believe. But in phenomenological interviewing, our role is not to agree or disagree—it is to learn as much as possible from those who have experienced the phenomenon. So, Fey's first rule of improvisation is important in our context as well. As we are moving through the dialogic back and forth among the participant's experiences of the phenomenon, our perspectives on the phenomenon, and the phenomenon itself, our job is to agree not with the other's perspectives, but with what they are opening up—how they are helping us gain access to a complex phenomenon. So when we find ourselves having negative or positive emotional responses to something a participant shares, these are often the best moments to bridle or post-reflex—as has been described in this book. These are the moments to make note of, to catch ourselves in, so they do not take hold of us and compromise our openness.

Just as in improvisation, then, we need to make sure we do not grind the interview to a halt. We need to be in-agreement-with whatever has been uttered by our "partner(s)" in the dialogue, so that we do our part in opening up the lived, felt, sensed nature(s) of the phenomenon.

Rule #2: *Not only to say yes, but* **YES, AND** *(You are supposed to agree and then add something of your own)*

In applying Fey's second rule of improvisation, it is important to stress that our responses, contributions to the dialogue, and follow up questions are all important to the ongoing and deepening understanding of the phenomenon. There is no way to know where this deepening will end up when we start. In this way Fey's rules for improvisation are entirely applicable to phenomenological interviewing. This rule is particularly important if we are crafting in-ness and through-ness phenomenological research, because the philosophical assumptions underlying these approaches are that all of us as researchers and participants are entering into what Heidegger referred to as a "conversation with the phenomenon."[2] And although Heidegger was talking about this philosophically, I think it can be readily used here when we are literally in-conversation-with research participants. We are in an improvised conversation in which we are producing something together. The difference is that we are responsible for learning more from them than they are from us. Nevertheless, approaching the interviews with the improvisational attitude that we are going to agree and say, "yes, and" helps us understand that we are contributing to what is produced in the interview event.

Rule #3: MAKE STATEMENTS *(Don't ask questions all the time)*

Although at first glance this might seem like the biggest stretch of the four rules, as we are going to be asking questions in an interview, after all, I think there are good reasons why this rule applies to phenomenological interviewing also. What Fey means, in her context, is to be confident and make contributions. The same holds in our context as well. It is important for the interviewer to be confident—to lead the dialogue, to develop a good feel for when to step in and when to hold back. Related to this point, Fey's "make statements" rule also helps us think about how we might phrase our questions/statements. In the flow of the conversation, sometimes we might be purposefully open, stating something such as "what was this experience like for you?", and other times more direct and specific—something such as "earlier you said that you were concerned and a bit nervous when you were about to begin your performance, tell me more about that." Finally, this particular rule can also remind us that our interviews can and often do become improvised conversations. Some of the most productive phenomenological interviews I have led have turned into conversations in which I am weaving statements and questions throughout, while the participant continues to tell her or his story. My weavings, in these cases, turn into nudges, "keep goings," and taps on the shoulder.

Rule #4: THERE ARE NO MISTAKES *(Only Opportunities)*

This is my favorite of Fey's rules of improvisation, and without a doubt the one with the greatest applicability to our context. Although others who write about how to conduct phenomenological interviews might disagree with me, I think it is incredibly important to view moments in which 1) we miss an opening to go deeper with the participant or 2) pose a follow-up question that leads the participant on a presumably irrelevant, to the phenomenon, tangent or 3) not redirect the participant back to the phenomenon as quickly as we might, not as mistakes but as opportunities.

I think approaching interviewing with this attitude is essential, especially when we are first developing our craft. I am not suggesting that we ignore moments when we could have done something else or when we missed an opening. Rather, I am asking that we treat these moments as inevitable outcomes of choosing to craft phenomenological research. For if we take the call for openness seriously, then there really is no possible way for us to avoid making mista ... I mean opportunities.

Observations

Although observations are not used as much as interviewing, I have found observations to be a very useful and worthwhile way to gather phenomenological data, especially if we situate our research as in-ness or through-ness. In in-ness and through-ness phenomenology, remember, the assumption is that phenomena move in and through human interactions with one another and other "objects" in the lifeworld. In this way, phenomena do not belong in the intentional consciousness of the experiencer (of-ness), they belong in the intentional relations circulating in the lifeworld of which each experiencer is a part. Therefore, I find observations to be a great way to gain some access to the way phenomena circulate among relations.

One activity I have had doctoral students and workshop participants do is something I call "phenomenology walks." In the phenomenological encounter below, I articulate the protocol I use.

Phenomenological Encounter #7
Phenomenology Walks

Purpose:
The purpose of a phenomenology walk is to see (where, what, how, and why) given phenomena might reside in various places.

Protocol:
Identify a location to start your walk. If you feel as though you are able to see a lot in this location, please stay. If you feel it is time to move on, please do so. (Caution: see note below).

1. Write down everything. Be a constant note-taker. Do not leave any stone unturned.
2. Ask yourself "wondering" questions. What is happening here? What is the purpose of this place? What conversations take place here? What practices take place here?
3. Draw upon your own understandings of phenomenological research.
4. Explore the ecological aspects of the place. Pay special attention to the cultures, discourses, systems, and everyday practices in this place.

After you complete your walk, you will need to return to your notes in order to write a journal entry. Your journal entry should include what you observed, what you think about it, and how you can use reading from the class and outside the class, if appropriate, to theorize it. It is not necessary to "cover" everything. In fact, please do not try to cover. Instead, locate a few things that you feel are poignant and then bring depth to them. As for length, I cannot imagine a substantive entry being any less than one and one-half single-spaced pages.

Note: When observing in this manner it is important to be ready for something to surprise you. When you think or feel as though there is nothing happening, first ask yourself what you might be missing. Sometimes some of the most mundane situations lead to the most interesting questions, ideas, and wonderings. Commit yourself to the patience this type of observation requires.

I think this course/workshop/lecture activity can be readily adapted and put to use when gathering data in a study. It is likely not necessary to follow all the specifications above (e.g., one and one-half single-spaced journal entry), however the protocol and perhaps less-polished journal entries that include questions, phrases, wonderings, drawings, etc., can not only serve as an important data-gathering tool, but also as a great opportunity to bridle and practice openness to the phenomenon. In addition, I think that using such an observation protocol can help us contextualize the phenomenon. This is especially important if you use Dahlberg et al.'s approach or my post-intentional approach. In in-ness—and, especially, in through-ness–oriented phenomenological research, we assume that phenomena do not exist in vacuums and that intentionalities run all over the place—in systems, in discourses, in the ways objects are arranged, for example in a room, in a theater, in home, in a classroom, in a hospital, on a street corner, in an art gallery, in a prison, and in practices. Making specific and explicit note of intentionalities in this manner is extremely important. I think taking pictures of spaces and places in which you think the phenomenon is being lived would be another good source of phenomenological data.

Sometimes what we observe and its significance might not come to us during the observation—when we are experiencing the phenomenon, so to speak, as the observer. It might come later, when we are removed from the observation event. It is important to give ourselves the mental and emotional space to understand that our dwelling with the phenomenon happens in and over time. This is an important purpose for phenomenology walks—to help us emotionally, mentally, and physically detach from the everyday worries and tasks (i.e., the natural attitude) and be more present in the phenomenological attitude. I close my discussion of observational data gathering with another phenomenological encounter, this time from Dr. Angel Pazurek. In her study (2013), she decided to extend the phenomenology walk, by enacting "phenomenology runs."

Phenomenological Encounter #8
Phenomenology RUNS

In his workshops and methodology courses, Vagle uses the pedagogical strategy of incorporating what he refers to as "phenomenological walks" as an activity to encourage learners to move beyond abstractly philosophizing about phenomenology and to additionally experience it and practice it.... This pedagogical exercise is designed to help practice phenomenological sensitivity or heightened awareness to identify everyday practices and phenomena we notice, or that which manifests itself to us in our being in the world.... This was a powerful activity for me in my scholarly development and was an exercise that impressed upon me the profound impact that an open sense of wonder could have on what becomes more visible to us as we move through the world when we make an effort to free ourselves from busy distractions and slow down in order to take note of that which surrounds us. It was at that point that I began to exercise a similar attentiveness in my online teaching and became increasingly captivated by how I saw engagement being manifested in shifting and changing ways in online learning environments for the adult learners I worked with in the online course I was teaching that became the context for this study. A similar heightened awareness, taking time to move through, yet free myself from other worldly distractions, became the way I approached my bridling process throughout this study as well and became the basis for my bridling plan. My phenomenological runs held great value in that they untethered me from my other obligations and afforded me the focus and increased time for metacognitive processing and attentive, thoughtful reflection necessary for effective bridling. I was able to conveniently document and record my thoughts using audio media and then upload the files I created to my online Tumblr blog that I had purposed as a multimedia-friendly online bridling journal.

Written Anecdotes

I think writing, in all sorts of forms, can serve as another useful way to gather phenomenological data. The formal writing protocol that I have seen stems from van Manen's lived experience description (LED) protocol. That said, I think a less formal writing protocol can be equally helpful in providing us with good access to the phenomenon and the myriad of intentional meanings that circulate through the lifeworld. With this in mind, I begin with van Manen's LED protocol, and then proceed to briefly discuss some less-structured ways to use writing.

In my 2006 study (Vagle 2006), I gave participants the choice to be interviewed or to write an LED about a moment they recognized and to which they responded when a student did not understand something during an instructional activity. Those who chose to write an LED were sent the following protocol.

Phenomenological Encounter #9
Lived Experience Description Protocol

The purpose of this protocol is for you to describe a specific time when you recognized and responded when a student did not understand something during an instructional activity. You are not asked to interpret how

---

you think teachers should teach, or to characterize your own teaching in general. The goal is to think about a specific moment. You can choose an everyday "run of the mill" experience. In other words, it does not have to be a "breakthrough" experience. Once you have chosen a specific moment to describe, consider the following guidelines (adapted from van Manen 2001) as you write.

1. Think about the event chronologically.
2. Describe what you saw, what was said, what you heard, how you felt, what you thought.
3. Try to describe the experience like you are watching it on film.
4. Describe the experience as you lived through it. Try to avoid causal explanations (this happened because ...), generalizations (this typically happens early in the morning), or abstract interpretations (I wonder if ...).
5. Write in a straightforward manner. Try to avoid beautifying your account with fancy phrases or flowery terminology.
6. If you want to use names in your description, please assign each person a pseudonym.
7. Read the example for guidance.

   With these suggestions in mind, please write a description in response to the following prompt.

Write a description of a time you recognized and responded to a student when he/she did not understand something during an instructional activity.

I also provided participants with an example. There was a fair amount of thought put into how to craft the example, as I wanted to live out van Manen's adapted protocol I had provided, but with a different phenomenon. My concern was that if the example was of the same phenomenon under investigation, that participants may explicitly or implicitly be drawn to "make theirs like the teacher's." I would encourage this or a similar plan for those who choose to follow this sort of protocol—especially if you choose to invoke of-ness or in-ness–oriented phenomenological research. Here are parts of an example of a completed LED from my study. I briefly circle back to this LED later in the chapter when describing how I analyzed the LEDs.

Phenomenological Encounter #10
Lived Experience Description (LED) from Participant (Kristine)

Every year I require that my eighth graders write a five-paragraph persuasive essay.... The assignment is to choose a controversial, arguable topic (arguable, of course, means that there are two valid sides to the argument) and construct a five-paragraph essay, using research, to persuade the reader to take the student's side.

I remember trying to help Amy come up with a [controversial] topic for her persuasive essay.... I encouraged her to ... come up with three broad, general reasons to support her opinion. She looked at me like I was crazy. "Well, it's just wrong. I don't have three reasons." I re-explained the structure of a five-paragraph essay, feeling like a broken record. I had gone over this several times in class, and no one had asked any questions then.

"You need to have three very broad reasons that you believe this, because then you'll narrow your argument down to nine specific examples that support your three main reasons." I tried very hard not to sound impatient. I don't mind explaining things to students more than once, but it bugs me when I present the information and no one asks questions. I understand that most students are probably self-conscious about asking questions in front of the whole class, but how do I help them get over that? I don't know.

I left Amy to think about this for awhile, and when I came back, she had changed her topic to abortion.

"Okay, that's your topic. Good. What's your thesis?" I asked, using the vocabulary that we'd practiced in class.

"Umm ... what's a thesis again?"

I re-explained the concept of a thesis as a statement of opinion.

"Yeah, okay. Abortion is wrong."

The thesis wasn't sophisticated or particularly well-written, but it was arguable. I decided this was a fine place to begin.

"Good. Now come up with your three main reasons. Do you know what I mean?" Amy assured me that she did.

I returned several minutes later, and her outline was blank.

"Do you need some help, Amy?"

"I can't remember what I'm supposed to do."

At this point, I brainstormed some reasons with her. I didn't know how else to explain to her how to come up with three main reasons—I had modeled this in class by writing a sample five-paragraph persuasive essay on the overhead, but that apparently hadn't been enough to help Amy understand. After I gave her one broad reason ("both the mother and the baby could be at risk for suffering from complications") and explained how we would then look for three specific examples of how abortions could be risky for both the mother and the baby, she seemed to understand. I told her to try to think of two more broad reasons that abortion is wrong.... At this point, I realized that I would have to do a lot more modeling next year.

As I continue to hone my craft, though, I also encourage the use of any form of writing that might open up the phenomenon. Although LEDs or something akin to them make very good sense when you want participants to write specifically about their experience of the phenomenon as a re-telling, there are many other purposes, for many other phenomena, in many other contexts. Poetry, short stories, fiction, realistic fiction, "three-minute" video scripts, narratives, and so on can also open up aspects of the phenomenon. I think this is especially the case in through-ness–oriented phenomenological research—the assumption is that phenomena and intentionalities are shifting, moving, undoing, and re-doing themselves in and over time through various, sometimes competing contexts. In order to capture these sorts of complexities, a more structured protocol might not be appropriate. Take this example from a narrative my daughter (when she was twelve years old and in the seventh grade) wrote for her Language Arts class, just after moving from Georgia to Minnesota in 2012.

Phenomenological Encounter #11
Maya's Narrative: A Finale of the Unforgettable

My lips were dry and cracked as I poured my heart out through the heavenly chorus of pre-teens' voices. I knew the song by heart. I had sung it about one billion times. I would spend some time in the shower singing until my voice was a mere whisper. Along with the obsessive humming while waiting for food at five guys and overdosing on youtube covers, the song was pretty much nailed into my head. I couldn't believe I was missing a professional theater camp for my all time favorite musical for a small community theater that was producing the fresh Off-Broadway hit *Freckleface Strawberry*.

To tell the truth, I would rather be here. Here, as in, a small theater in Watkinsville, Georgia. It was mid-afternoon and I was still energetic despite the hardship of singing and dancing. I was in the, from my point of view, legendary Civic Center, that was the center for all group events and OYP musicals. The green, and perhaps a little blue, seats were almost filled, the general audience being in the center like bees circling around their hive. I guess they wanted to see better, or maybe that was just a random coincidence.

Anyways, the theater itself was musty with its stone walls and humdrum lights illuminating the nearly invisible stairs. The stage was dirty and the ghosts of duct tape lines marked the beaten-down area. Ignoring the fact that it was not the best place, appearance wise, I would rather be here, with my performing arts studio, OYP, with all my friends and the people that had trained me to be the singer and performer I was.

My mind shifted back to the song, and as I sang, I could smell the person standing to the right of me sweating and I could see the whole cast grinning from ear to ear. It felt kind of silly to do this, I mean aren't we supposed to be more mature and stuff? I decided to grin along with them, enjoying the moment of childhood and making a mental note to still keep a part of this moment inside my head. I suddenly felt less distracted and more focused on singing and making it memorable. As a wise and rather knowledgeable performer once told me:

"You must be alive and present when you are performing. Pretend that electricity is circulating through your body, energizing your very being."

I was present. I was alive. The energy was flowing through my body. I could taste the anticipation in the air to see the crowd's reaction. I licked my lips in thought of making them less dry and barren. I could sense my make up slowly melting off. I straightened my flower patterned pencil skirt and my blue blazer. I was poised for the ending of the song and dressed for success. I had been playing a teacher—a creativity-obsessed teacher not to mention.

As the last song ended, I was left satisfied and rather energetic. My mind raced and I think I lost some brain cells from all the applause. One of the directors came up to the corner of the stage I was standing in. I grimaced at the sudden thought coming on. I guess it was unfortunate that right now out of all the time in the world I would have thought of the horrid fact. Tonight was my last night in Georgia. My last night at home. I pushed the disturbing thought out of my mind and focused on what the director was saying.

"Well, I would like to thank . . ." The director, Shane Hannon, rambled on listing different people who helped with the sacred art of performing.

A good five minutes later, Shane was on the set crew, thanking numerous dads. A couple of days ago, I had helped paint some of the set. Oh, the old days. My mind flitted through memories of rehearsals, learning music, failing dance at dance moves, and figuring out how to act. We clapped for the lights and accompaniment, and finally, the curtains prepared to close. Or that's what I thought they would do.

Instead, they remained open and Shane glanced down at the paper he was holding.

"I would like to say some things about the teacher over here." He motioned to me and I nervously chugged up to the front corner with him. He held me close, wrapping one arm around me and the other holding the paper that was dangling loosely at his side. He pressed down on his yellow Freckleface Strawberry shirt and gave me a reassuring smile. I slowly smiled back, me on the brink of tears. He talked to the audience about me playing the teacher and how I had been at OYP for a long time. I held a record there and how much I loved it.

Then of course there was the purpose he was doing this. I was moving all the way across the country. My body reacted as I shivered and fought even more to hold back tears. It hurt so much to think of leaving. I could see the sad faces of my parents and numerous adults I had gotten to know. One mom snapped a half-hearted picture and another wiped her eye and gave the whole cast a look of sympathy.

As Shane continued, he rambled on about how I had been in ten productions and if I hadn't been leaving, it would have been a higher number. A good ten minutes later he ended with a final squeeze and suggested an encore. A couple girls pulled me to center stage and we sang a reprise of the song and the curtain closed as the cast gathered in a big, wet circle of sweaty and over-emotional thespians.

> I still tear up when I think of this memory. I guess it's because of the mixing of emotions in the story. The fact that my farewell was an announcement on a stage was so special and so unique that it was unbearable.
>
> Following up on that, I think that I wanted to tell this story because I needed to let go of all the emotions trapped inside me and just express myself.
>
> I think I have also changed a bit since then. In the following week, I was depressed and sad and I could not get a grip on the fact that it was over. Now, I'm perfectly fine and not feeling majorly sad at all.
>
> I can't say it wasn't an educational experience. I learned a lot. I realized that I had faithful friends that believed in me! I hadn't realized how lucky I was until then. Maybe, someday I'll be able to tell them that.

Just because Maya's narrative was not written in response to a structured phenomenological research protocol does not mean that it does not provide rich and important openings for phenomenological analysis—in this case about the phenomenon, "in-moving, in-leaving." Sometimes letting writers just write provides even "better" phenomenological data. Other times, asking writers to write a number of short episodic writings over time in various contexts might be of more use. Here is where I think turning to arts-based methodologies (e.g., Cahnmann-Taylor & Siegsemund 2008) is a good course of action.

Arts-Based Methodologies: Photo-Elicitation, Visual and Performance Arts

Arts-based methodological tools are effective at enabling participants to articulate what they consider relevant to their experiences (Marquez-Zenkov 2007). Visual sociologists have used image-based "photo elicitation" techniques to access adolescents' insights in ways language-centered methods cannot (Raggl and Schratz 2004). The visual arts draw on and develop abilities to observe, envision, and explore beyond usual conceptions and capacities and reflect on that process (Hetland, Winner, Veenema, and Sheridan 2007).

In my current post-intentional phenomenological study, photo-elicitation is the central data-gathering technique. In this phenomenological encounter, I reflect on my perspectives engaging teachers in a professional development experience prior to designing the study, as I came to identify the phenomenon.

Phenomenological Encounter #12
Social Class-Sensitive Photo-Storying: Middle-Class (Messy) Affordances

After framing the purposes of photo-elicitation and photo-storying, I displayed this photo of my messy garage.

Figure 6.1

I could sense a bit of awkwardness as participants looked at the picture. I perceived some as shocked—this picture seemed to disrupt their assumption of what my garage did or should look like. And although my self-deprecating humor lightened the mood considerably, the group could not escape the obvious mess in the picture. As the group moved from laughter to substantive interpretation of this space, the dialogue was tentative. I began to tell stories about particular aspects of the photo—how much I loved the versatile orange ladder in the upper left and how proud I was of my middle son Rhys who learned to ride a bike without training wheels at age 4 and now had graduated to the bike in the foreground of the photo. The participants seemed deeply engaged in this story-telling, yet one participant was brave enough to point out that this is a pretty messy garage and that there was no way she could live with a garage like this. Others agreed. I also offered that my personality—being a big picture, theorizing type—often made the consistent detailed work of keeping a garage clean next to overwhelming.

And others, then, seemed to start to feel bad for me—maybe embarrassed even. One suggested that my garage was this messy because I was so busy as a professor, implying that if I were not as busy, that my garage would not be so messy, that I would have more time to clean it regularly. This particular point provided an important opening into what I have termed "middle-classed affordances." I asked why I was being afforded this? And followed by wondering whether the same affordances would be given to the families of their students—the homes and yards we had all watched from the school bus windows as we drove in and out of their students' neighborhoods on the bus ride school administration led us on two months prior? On that bus ride we saw a lot of "stuff" in yards, under an overhang that was to act as a garage, sometimes covered by a large tarp, other times not. I reminded the group that in the whole-faculty debrief of the bus ride we had attributed "messiness" in yards to lower socio-economic status—that such messiness signaled homes and perhaps lives being rundown, in turmoil, and I added, was a sign of less civility.

Now, however, my garage was being afforded other explanations. The messiness that was obvious in the photograph was interpreted in much more nuanced, complex ways, and much more graciously. I challenged the group to afford the students and the families in their community the same. What if those "run down" houses with the messy yards were interpreted in similar ways as my garage was interpreted? What if teachers started to wonder more about the daily lives of their students and families? Which families' lives might be as busy or much busier than mine—parents working two or three shifts at one of the poultry factories, other families with both workers temporarily unemployed during the greatest recession since the Great Depression.

The group considered such matters, not all that loudly but seemingly in a contemplative way, as one participant turned the group's attention back to the photograph, this time suggesting that we focus on the garage door, backgrounded and to the right. The participant suggested that I was also being afforded something else that others in the community might not be afforded: I can shut my garage door. No one could really "see" my messiness. A seemingly new literal and metaphorical understanding had emerged—folks from working class and poor backgrounds may not have a garage door to shut.

In the photo-storying study Angela Coffee, Colleen Clements and I are now crafting, there are many photos being taken and interpreted, for many purposes. Given that the phenomenon focuses on how this pedagogical tool serves as a means to create social class-sensitive teaching and learning environments, arranging many photo-storying enactments over time is important. These photo-stories become glimpses of how the phenomenon is tentatively and momentarily lived, and equally important is that the visual and linguistic access to the phenomenon deepens what might be thinkable and possible to learn about the phenomenon. In other words, the data-gathering tool is generative. I have found the same to hold with the use of music as a data-gathering tool.

I spend time discussing Dr. Joseph Pate's post-intentional study (Pate 2012) in chapter 8, as it focuses specifically on music listening as a phenomenon, and since of course the use of music as a data-gathering tool is central to his study. Here I want to emphasize a process I use to help us engage with music when data gathering. This process could be used in any phenomenological study as a way to open up the aesthetic qualities of a phenomenon. Music has a way to draw listeners into full engagement and tends to activate emotive aspects of phenomena that may or may not be evoked without it. Further, I strongly favor multiple interactions with songs—through listening, reading, and observing. With this in mind, I now describe the process I have used with one song in particular: *Jar of Hearts* by Christina Perri (2010) (http://www.youtube.com/watch?v=8v_4O44sfjM). I was introduced to this song by my daughter, Maya, a few years back when she was trying to select a song for a talent show she planned to enter. From my first listen, I was drawn to this song. I am not exactly sure why, but ever since my introduction to the song I have used it to help demonstrate the multilayered ways phenomenological data can be gathered from one source, and how musical expressions always already contain this multilayerdness.

Phenomenological Encounter #13
Experiencing "Jar of Hearts"

The following process, of course, can be used with any song—assuming that you have access to the music video and lyrics associated with the song.

Set-up

I set up the process simply by prefacing the power of music much like I just did in setting up this encounter. I then ask participants to take notes about what they think, feel, sense, and are reminded of. Sometimes I ask them to identify potential phenomena that they interpret as circulating through the song, others times I do not. This is appropriate given the nature of the process/activity. If one were to apply this to a study, the phenomena would already be identified. In this case, one would be entering the experience with the song by focusing on her or his interpretations of how the phenomenon under investigation might be circulating in and through the song. I ask participants to write in any way that makes sense to them—as long as they know what they meant, wondered about, and interpreted later when they return to their journal.

We then listen to the song three times.

Listen #1—Just the Song

During listen #1, we just listen to the song without lyrics or the video. We don't talk during this time. We just listen and write. I have noticed that some prefer to listen and not write at all until they have experienced the entire song. Others write as they are listening. I often see a few participants with their eyes closed throughout, while I perceive others as having distant looks. After the song is over we write for a few minutes, and then ready ourselves for listen #2. We don't discuss our interpretations yet.

Listen #2—The Song with Lyrics

During listen #2, we listen to the same song again, but this time we see the lyrics projected as in karaoke. We follow the same process, but now we add the layer of textual analysis. Again, some students choose to wait

---

until the song is complete before writing, and after the song is over we write for a few minutes. As with listen #1, we don't discuss our interpretations at this point.

Listen #3—The Song with the Music Video

During listen #3, we listen to the same song again, but this time we see the music video performed as well. Now we have embodied representation and performance of meanings. We follow the same process of listening and writing. After everyone has had the opportunity to finish writing we then begin our discussion.

Discussion

Although the discussion takes different shape with each group, we generally focus on the different things we learned, wondered about, etc., with each different modality. We talk about the multiple layers and complexities, and talk about what each modality affords and does not afford. Inevitably, participants report that their understandings and insights changed each time they listened, in part because of the repetition and in part because of the modality. We dig most deeply into the third listen and find that the musical, embodied, choreographed performance opens up meanings that the song itself cannot accomplish. At the same time, when we see the performance this can limit other possible interpretations. We need to remind ourselves that there are multiple possible interpretations of art, and as one interpreter, our intentional relations with the art can take many different shapes in and over time. We are not trying to figure out what the artist "meant," we are trying to see some of the innumerable meanings that might show themselves through the art.

There are of course, many other possibilities including but not limited to films, other dramatizations and re-enactments, and works of visual art. I think being as creative as possible is important, and do not assume that just because you have not seen a particular data gathering tool used in a phenomenological study, that it is off limits. I encourage you to explore all options.

How are Phenomenological Data Analyzed?

In phenomenological research, like other qualitative research methodologies, it is difficult to separate data gathering from analysis, as the two are so delicately intertwined throughout all phases of a study. That said, as I indicated in chapter 4, this is one methodological matter in which there is quite a bit of consistency across phenomenological research approaches—even though the names for steps differ and some of the philosophical underpinnings for each approach necessitate some nuances. All phenomenological research approaches that are routinely practiced have a substantive commitment to a whole-part-whole analysis method. In short, whole-part-whole analysis methods stem from the idea that we must always think about focal meanings (e.g., moments) in relation to the whole (e.g., broader context) from which they are situated—and once we begin to remove parts from one context and put them in dialogue with other parts, we end up creating new analytic wholes that have particular meanings in relation to the phenomenon. I illustrate this process below.

Based on my reading of the data analysis practices in phenomenological research, I address this question by first articulating the way I employ a whole-part-whole analysis method in my post-intentional approach. This also means I do not spend as much time discussing it in chapter 8 when I more fully explicate post-intentional methodology. I am not suggesting that those who choose other approaches should necessarily follow my lead. However, I want to articulate whole-part-whole in an accessible way so the gist is grasped on an introductory level. Then, I expect that you will need to make some choices about how you will particularize your analytic process based on whether you decide to conduct more descriptive-oriented or interpretive-oriented phenomenological research. With this in mind, I have included a phenomenological encounter where I highlight the steps various high-amplitude phenomenologists have used in their particular approaches.

Before proceeding, though, I think it is necessary to pause and address an important data-gathering/analysis matter. Many qualitative methodologists emphasize the importance of triangulation in order to more fully justify claims, and therefore increase the validity of any themes, assertions, categories, etc. The term triangulation appears to be rooted in celestial navigation of the seas. That is, triangulating coordinates would help guide a ship as it sails. In qualitative research methodologies, triangulation has been used as a metaphor to represent how you might find the "coordinates" from multiple data sources in order to "find" findings. Although I think this concept has some applicability to phenomenological research, I am concerned that such a practice might make the analysis more mechanistic than I prefer. For me, in phenomenological research, when we have multiple data moments such as interviews, writings, and observations from a number of participants, over a period of time, I do not think one needs to triangulate across these moments in order to say something meaningful. Sometimes a single statement, from one participant, at one moment in time is so powerful that it needs to be amplified. Another time, there might be convergence across multiple data moments and this contextual variation, as Dahlberg, Dahlberg, and Nystrom (2008) like to call it, provides deep and rich insights into a particular shape the phenomenon has taken. In both cases (the single moment or the multiple moments), what we craft is equally important to the final representation.

Another related matter associated with the question of triangulation is whether it is wise to use a computer software program such as NVIVO

(QSR International) to analyze phenomenological data. My stance on this is similar to my stance on triangulation. Although I see some of its merit, I worry about it producing mechanistic representations rather than a deeply embodied crafting. That said, I also do not want to be an absolutist about this particular matter. So, my advice to those wondering is this: if a program such as NVIVO helps you, then use it. If it feels uncomfortable and stifling, then do not.

Data-Analysis Underpinnings/Assumptions

As with all phenomenological work, data should be analyzed based on the type of approach you are using. As I described earlier in this section, descriptive phenomenological researchers following Giorgi tend to proceed in particular ways, interpretive folks following van Manen in other ways, and of course there is overlap between the two. And others, like me, don't like to commit to one way or the other, and instead move across boundaries. Nevertheless, here a few commitments I think are important in all phenomenological analyses.

1. Whole-parts-whole process
2. A focus on intentionality and not subjective experience
3. A balance among verbatim excerpts, paraphrasing, and your descriptions/interpretations
4. An understanding that you are crafting a text—not merely coding, categorizing, making assertions and reporting

I now articulate the whole-part-whole process I like to use and then outline a few other analysis protocols that you might find useful. You will see in my process a marked route for proceeding, but it is relatively simple. I do this because I find that some guidance is good, but too much can stultify the creativity necessary to craft high-amplitude phenomenological texts.

Step 1: Holistic Reading of Entire Text
The first read of the data should involve getting attuned to the whole data collection event (e.g., transcript, description, observation, fictional writing). At this point, I suggest that the researcher not take notes and simply spend some time getting reacquainted with the data.

Step 2: First Line-by-Line Reading
I then tend to move to a series of line-by-line readings. The first line-by-line reading should include careful note taking and marking of excerpts that appear to contain initial meanings. I place parentheses around large chunks of text and make margin notes that might be questions (e.g., How does this

influence her recognition of [the student's] understanding?) at times and statements (e.g., potential meaning "having an idea in your head") at other times. I have found it helpful to turn to my journal in order to explicate some of my thoughts. This is an example of bridling, because it allows one to harness what is being read and thought. This did not mean that we can totally set aside our own presuppositions, but it does mean that we try to own them, so to speak, and interrogate how they might influence the analysis.

Step 3: Follow-Up Questions

Once we have read the whole transcript/description/observation and have completed the first line-by-line reading of one transcript/description/observation, I suggest proceeding to read each of the others in the same manner. I would then review margin notes in order to craft follow-up questions for each participant. The questions should be designed to clarify intentional meanings that one predicts, at the early stages of analysis, might be important to describe/interpret/represent the phenomenon.

Step 4: Second Line-by-Line Reading

The second line-by-line reading should involve articulating the meanings, based on the markings, margin notes, and the follow-up with research participants. I often first complete this step by hand, although this would not be necessary, and then copy and paste electronically each participant's identified excerpts or parts of their transcript/description/observation to a new document. The new document (one for each individual participant) would then contain all of the potential parts that the researcher thinks might contribute to the phenomenological text.

Step 5: Third Line-by-Line Reading

This will then lead to a third line-by-line reading in which you can articulate your analytic thoughts about each part. Continue this process with each participant's interview/description/observation until you have articulated the analytic thoughts for each part for each participant.

Step 6: Subsequent Readings

Subsequent readings should now involve reading across individual participants' data, with the goal of looking for what I am now calling "tentative manifestations" that van Manen would most likely call "themes," Dahlberg "patterns of meaning," and Giorgi "meaning units" and then "invariant structures." Once you begin to see tentative manifestations you should give the tentative manifestations preliminary titles. Throughout this process you will most likely notice new things and therefore add and delete analytic thoughts.

Often it is helpful to see a glimpse of what this might actually look like in action. I return to Kristine's LED from earlier in the chapter to demonstrate what this might look like when enacted. After my holistic reading of Kristine's LED, I settled into line-by-line readings. I noted some chunks of text that stood out to me—I wanted to learn more about them. Here is one in particular that I wanted to explore more deeply.

> Kristine: She looked at me like I was crazy. "Well, it's just wrong. I don't have three reasons." I re-explained the structure of a five-paragraph essay, feeling like a broken record. I had gone over this several times in class, and no one had asked any questions then.

In my bridling journal I began to wonder more about what this was like for Kristine, and then stepped back to consider the phenomenon, recognizing and responding when students do not understand. I wrote:

> A couple things here.... First, "seeing the student" as looking at the teacher like she was crazy is laced with intersubjectivity—having a look means that the student thinks or feels a certain way. The look, however, is also tied together with the statement. I wonder how the perception would have been perceived if the look and the words were separated somehow? The teacher's response is also important, especially the feeling of frustration that is stressed through the "broken record" analogy and the emphasis placed on "then." This is quite important.

In my follow-up questions to Kristine, I posed two in relation to this chunk of text. Here are the two questions and Kristine's responses:

> **How did you come to know the student's look as a look like you are "crazy"?**
>
> It's the classic middle school look—teachers get it all the time! At first glance it looks simply like a blank look, but upon further scrutiny there is a touch of disdain, maybe a little boredom, and definitely a little bit of "I'm just tolerating you because I have no choice."
>
> **What is it like to feel "like a broken record" during your instruction?**
>
> I would say that that's one of the reasons I left teaching (I did, after six years, to pursue a library science degree). I am not one of those people who talks just to hear themselves talk—when I was presenting/instructing in front of the class, what I was saying, was important to the assignment. It drove me crazy when I had to repeat things two or three times, and then ten more times again individually because kids weren't paying attention. I realize that a little bit of that is expected, I do. And maybe because I just can't tolerate that, teaching isn't the place for me! I am a

> very conscientious, focused person, and I expected my students to be the same. They just all weren't.

Based on my initial analysis and Kristine's responses to my questions, I felt that this aspect of her LED provided important access to the phenomenon. In order to not lose sight of its saliency, I proceeded in my third, fourth, and subsequent reads to put this chunk of text, my bridled interpretations, and Kristine's responses in dialogue with other chunks of text from other participants in other data moments.

> Kurt: It was then that I recognized a lack of understanding in what I was doing. As I was solving the problem, students were quiet ... too quiet. They were utterly confused. I started to feel a little frustrated and even aggravated! How come these students can't understand this? It really isn't *that* hard! It was as if they had forgotten all of the stuff they had already learned. I began to hear comments like. "I'm lost!", "I don't get it," "What are you talking about?", and, of course, "Is this going to be on the test?"
>
> While frustration is present in Kurt's description, there is also a sense of disbelief and amazement. "It really isn't *that* hard!" Being amazed by a student's lack of understanding presents itself often. Lacy described being amazed that her grade seven science students did not understand how oxygen travels through the body in blood cells, and how she questioned her own teaching as a result.
>
> Lacy: I'm just like, oh my god, how could they not know that? Am I that bad of a teacher that they can't figure that out or that I haven't gotten that across, I just don't understand how we could have missed such an important concept or that that didn't come across.
>
> This sense of being amazed or perhaps shocked when students do not understand might accompany a feeling that students should understand based on how much time was spent preparing students to understand.
>
> Kristine: She looked at me like I was crazy. "Well, it's just wrong. I don't have three reasons." I re-explained the structure of a five-paragraph essay, feeling like a broken record. I had gone over this several times in class, and no one had asked any questions *then*.
>
> Kristine's feeling here (like a broken record, her emphasis on *then*) are tied to her perceptions of the student's look (like Kristine was crazy). There is a hint of frustration here as well. For the teacher, it seems that the idea that students do not understand when the teacher and the students have been working with certain concepts is frustrating, aggravating, and surprising to teachers. While these feelings are not the end, per se, of what it is like to recognize and respond when students do not understand, these feelings certainly are an essential part of what it is like for teachers to be recognizing their students' understanding.

It is important to note that this is but one example from one chunk of text, from one study. I have since followed the same whole-part-whole process I have articulated here, but have applied it somewhat differently depending on the phenomenon and, of course, my growth as a phenomenological craftsperson. So, as you get started or continue to grow in your own craft it is important to make nuanced changes in response to your phenomenon, the approach you are drawn to, and what feels most comfortable to you. With this in mind, the following phenomenological encounter outlines other step-by-step ways to carry out phenomenological analysis. I encourage you to go to these resources directly in order to gain deeper insights for how these craftspeople carry out their unique approaches to analysis.

Phenomenological Encounter #14
Phenomenological Analysis Options
Van Manen: Hermenuetic Phenomenology Thematic Analysis

van Manen (2001)

Isolating Thematic Statements—Three Approaches (pp. 92–93)

Wholistic

Attend to the text as a whole and ask, What sententious (i.e., full of meaning, terse statement of sentiment) phrase may capture the fundamental meaning or main significance of the text as a whole? Try to express that meaning by formulating such a phrase.

Selective (Highlighting)

Listen to or read a text several times and ask, What statement(s) or phrase(s) seem particularly essential or revealing about the phenomenon or experience being described? Circle, underline, or highlight these statements.

Detailed (Line-by-Line)

Look at every single sentence or sentence cluster and ask, What does this sentence or sentence cluster reveal about the phenomenon or experience being described?

(See pp. 94–95 for examples of these processes)

Moustakas—Descriptive Phenomenological Research

(Taken from McNamara 2005)

Moustakas' (1994) modiþcation of Van Kaam's method of phenomenological data analysis:

---

1. Listing and preliminary grouping of meaningful statements.
2. Reduction and elimination to determine invariant constituents.
3. Clustering of invariant constituents.
4. Final identifcation of the invariant constituents by application—validation.
5. Individual textural description.
6. Individual structural description.
7. Textural-structural description.

Crotty (1996)

(Note: Crotty (1996) does not appear to necessarily create his own phenomenological analysis method. Rather he reviews and in turn critiques various ways nursing researchers have conducted phenomenological analyses. He concludes that nursing researchers have adopted and/or adapted from three sources in particular [Colaizzi 1978 ; Giorgi 1985; and van Kaam 1966]. Given that I have already described Giorgi's in this text, the Colaizzi and van Kaam are described here.).

A Colaizzi-Style Method:

1. Reading the descriptions.
2. Extracting "significant statements."
3. Formulating meanings.
4. Organizing formulated meanings into clusters of themes.
5. Exhaustively describing the investigated phenomenon.
6. Validating the exhaustive description by each respondent.

A van Kaam-Style Method:

1. Listing descriptive expressions, their preliminary grouping into categories, and ranking categories by frequency of occurrence.
2. Reducing descriptive expressions to more precise terms.
3. Eliminating irrelevant expressions or elements.
4. Formulating a hypothetical identification of the phenomenon.
5. Applying the hypothetical description to randomly chosen cases of the sample, revising the hypothetical description in the light of this testing, and retesting on further samples.
6. Finally identifying the description.

In closing my response to the question of data analysis and to this chapter overall, I think it is important to be reminded of something Linda Finlay (2008b, 5-6) writes:

When it comes to analysis, phenomenological researchers engage in active and sustained reflection as they "dwell" with the data and interrogate it, for example asking: "If a person has said this, what does this suggest of their experience of the world?" ... [some] researchers prefer to use open, spontaneous, fluid dialogue in a group context rather than adhering to any explicit procedures. Whichever the approach, researchers are involved in "an extreme form of care that savors the situations described in a slow, meditative way and attends to, even magnifies, all the details." (Wertz 2005, 172)

I really like this way of thinking about analysis. As I have stated throughout this text, there are many approaches and ways of crafting phenomenological research. This is one of the many reasons why I see this as a craft more than a method. As phenomenologists, we are actively engaged in crafting something, and as we engage in craftwork, we need to resist the urge to follow a recipe and, instead, embrace the open searching, tinkering, and reshaping that this important work requires. With this in mind, I close section 2 with another resource dig.

Resource Dig (Section 2)
Methodology

In this resource dig, I have included some methodologically-oriented resources across the various phenomenological research approaches that I have emphasized in this section. That said, I hold the post-intentional resources for the end of section 3. As with the philosophical resource dig, this dig is neither exhaustive nor inclusive. I have made choices about methodological resources I emphasize here and again include more in the *additional resources* section of the book. What is included below and at the end of the book should provide plenty of possibilities—and of course in each of these resources there are many more resources that you may find helpful. Enjoy your digging.

Texts

Methodology Books

Throughout section 2 of the book, I have discussed Dahlberg et al., Giorgi, and van Manen at some length. Here I list a few more methodology books that have been particularly useful to phenomenological craftswomen and men.

Moustakas, C. 1994. *Phenomenological research methods.* Thousand Oaks: Sage.

Moustakas' work is very well-grounded philosophically, theoretically, and methodologically, and has been a resource for crafting phenomenological research for many years. Although Moustakas' field of study is psychology, his method can be applied to any field. I think those interested in of-ness descriptive-oriented phenomenological research would find Moustakas' approach quite useful, and those who want to emphasize an in-ness or through-ness approach may find it necessary to pick and choose aspects.

Pollio, H., T. B. Henley, and C. J. Thompson. 2006. *The phenomenology of everyday life.* New York: Cambridge University Press.

Pollio et al.'s work does a particularly good job tying philosophy and methodology, and then illustrating how various phenomenological studies following their method can take shape. The majority of the book includes a number of examples. Like Moustakas, Pollio et al. is situated primarily in psychology, and also like Moustakas, would be useful for those across fields. As for approach, I read Pollio as descriptive and interpretive. So, I think those interested in descriptive and interpretive approaches would likely find much of this resource instructive, less so for those interested in post-intentional phenomenology.

Smith, J. A., P. Flowers, and M. Larkin. 2009. *Interpretive phenomenological analysis; Theory, method, and research.* London: Sage.

As the title clearly indicates, Smith, Flowers, and Larkin's text is situated in a hermeneutic phenomenology tradition. They do an excellent job grounding their methodology in the philosophy and then walk the reader through their analysis procedure—often referred to in short as IPA. They provide many helpful resources and illustrations of how to craft an IPA-based study. I perceive their work to be most useful to those interested in crafting hermeneutic (in-ness) phenomenological studies, but those interested in "of-ness" and "through-ness" studies might find aspects appealing as well.

Methodology Articles

There are many articles (see Additional Resources) that can serve as good methodological resources. I selected the three below not because they are necessarily more useful than the others, but because I think they make the methodological/analytical matter of researcher reflexivity in phenomenology concrete, methodologically, while keeping it closely connected to underlying philosophies.

Finlay, L. 2008a. A dance between the reduction and reflexivity: Explicating the phenomenological psychological attitude. *Journal of Phenomenological Psychology* 39:1–32.

I have found this particular article to be helpful in making sense of both the philosophical and methodological nuanced differences between the phenomenological reduction—or bracketing—and researcher reflexivity—Dahlberg's bridling being one example.

Vagle, M.D., H. E. Hughes, and D. J. Durbin. 2009. Remaining skeptical: Bridling for and with one another. *Field Methods* 21(4): 347–367

Often researcher reflexivity is thought of as solely an individual researcher's examination of her or his relationship with a phenomenon. In this article, we set out to demonstrate how bridling can also be practiced on research teams—where one's reflexivity is made public to co-researchers, thus making the interrogation of assumptions, pre-understandings, and so on, potentially deeper and more nuanced.

A Post-Intentional Approach to Phenomenological Research

In this final section of the book we will work our way through the following important questions:

1. In post-intentional phenomenology, how are particular aspects of post-structural philosophy put in dialogue with phenomenological philosophies? **(Chapter 7)**
2. How can those interested in crafting post-intentional phenomenological research proceed methodologically through my five-component process? **(Chapter 8)**
3. What are some of the ways in which post-intentional phenomenology has been put into practice? **(Chapter 9)**

As I have stated throughout, I close this book with an approach I have developed and now use when I craft phenomenological research. This section is a bit shorter than sections 1 and 2, not because I am less passionate about it—the opposite actually—but because I have covered a fair amount of the necessary ground already. For example, in section 1 I discussed the importance of tentative manifestations and through-ness, as opposed to of-ness and in-ness, in my approach. In section 2, I discussed tools and strategies for crafting phenomenological research that I think are equally applicable to my approach—hence, I do not re-describe these tools and strategies at the same depth in this section. Instead, I have built on my earlier foreshadowings in the book in order to articulate clearly my post-intentional phenomenological approach. As with the first two sections, I close this section with a resource dig, with particular emphasis on examples of post-intentional phenomenological studies. I begin with the philosophy.

Post-Intentional Phenomenology

The Philosophical Underpinnings

I now see myself as a phenomenological craftsperson who has grown to have some sort of mysterious attraction to post-structuralism—someone who tinkers with post-ideas in his craft. Although this tinkering feels a bit dangerous, perhaps this speaks to my mysterious attraction to things that are supposedly "anti-phenomenological" (Ihde 2003) while also saying that I do, in fact, "do" phenomenology. I like these in between spaces—the spaces that one is not supposed to go, not only because one is not supposed to go or be there, but because I think some of the most generative and radical philosophical, theoretical, and methodological work in qualitative research writ large and, in my case, phenomenological research, happens when we as phenomenological craftswomen and men situate ourselves on the edges of things.

In order to clearly explicate how I am imagining post-intentional phenomenology, philosophically, I zero in on how "old"[1] phenomenology from the days of Husserl, Heidegger, Merleau-Ponty, Sartre, Gadamer and others was indeed radical and how "new" phenomenology can be equally, if not more, radical than the old. I suggest, as I discussed to some extent in section 1, that the old phenomenology was countering centuries of philosophy that situated meaning, knowing, and being in Descartes' stable self, subject, and consciousness, and in doing so, swathed a path, as we would say where I grew up in rural Minnesota, for all sorts of other philosophies to follow.

I also suggest that the old phenomenology should not be discarded, nor should phenomenology be positioned today as if it is that same phenomenology from yesteryear. It can be imagined as a different phenomenology—a bunch of gnarly branches banging into one another—and that gnarliness gives it potential for radical punch.

Post-Intentional Phenomenology: The Basis for a Political Philosophy

I have introduced my conception of a post-intentional phenomenology elsewhere (Vagle 2010a,b) by suggesting that a post-structural commitment such as seeing knowledge as partial, situated, endlessly deferred, and circulating through relations would be a most helpful way to reconceive phenomenological research today. This sort of "loosening up" would allow for a more nuanced reading of lived experience and would embrace the important philosophizing and theorizing that has taken place since the old phenomenology (Ihde 2003) broke this ground a century or so ago. In this chapter, I develop those earlier ideas a bit more fully by drawing on Ihde's (2003) argument for *post-phenomenology*[2] in order to "post" what I consider to be the most important phenomenological contribution to Western philosophy—intentionality.

Posting Intentionality

To briefly review from section 1, the philosophical use of intentionality is often, and almost always actually, in the US at least, confused with how the word "intend" is used in US English—that is, to refer to one's purpose or plan for doing something. In phenomenological philosophy beginning with Husserl (1970[1936]) and extending through Heidegger (1998[1927]), Merleau-Ponty (1964[1947]), and Sartre (in Moran and Mooney 2002), to name a few phenomenological philosophers influential in this respect, intentionality has been used to describe the way in which humans are connected meaningfully with the world. Whatever the image, phenomenologists must understand that they are not studying the subjective intentions, as in purposes or objectives, of individuals but the ways meanings "come-to-be" in relations. This becomes incredibly difficult to do, and for others to trust when we, as phenomenological craftswomen and men, use empirical frames to try to make sense of intentionality.

In order to "post" intentionality, it is first necessary to recast some of the old phenomenology—not because it is no longer useful as a whole, but because particular aspects of it can, at once, be read as a carry-over of the egocentric predicament and as missing some important opportunities for growth. I agree with Ihde's (2003) concern that Husserl's use of words such as ego, consciousness, and subjectivity can actually reify the very thing Husserl was trying to resist. So, although Husserl was doing something mighty radical at the time, he did not break free enough from the language and meanings that had crystallized since Descartes. And more importantly, most critiques of phenomenology conflate phenomenology writ large with Husserlian phenomenology, failing to dig deep enough to see all the various ways in which phenomenology has grown and changed over the years. Of equal concern, to me at least, is that many present-day phenomenological philosophers (Ihde excluded) such as Sokolowski and leading phenomenological researchers like Giorgi (e.g., 1997) hold on to Husserl, even though we can see some modifications in Giorgi's most recent work. This is not to say that there is not still much to be gained by going with Husserl. The problem lies, again, in conflating Husserl's phenomenology and all things phenomenological. Ihde (2003) goes so far as to say "The very notion, 'subjectivity,' carries with it the in-the-box signification. And I [he] contend[s] that this signification cannot be escaped so long as the old vocabulary is used" (p. 11).

The "in-the-box signification" that Ihde (2003) mentions points to the same concern Sokolowski (2000) holds when referring to the egocentric predicament. The key difference between Ihde and Sokolowski, however, is that Ihde departs from the very ideas that continually resignify a subject-centered phenomenology, and by virtue of his departure helps phenomenology continue to, in turn, help Western thought work its way out of its egocentric predicament. Two moves Ihde makes in arguing for a postphenomenology have been particularly useful to my development of a post-intentional phenomenology. I briefly describe these two moves and use them to "post" intentionality.

First, Ihde (2003) substitutes embodiment for subjectivity, crediting Merleau-Ponty for stressing that bodies are our access to the world and one another and that bodies cannot be transcendental, only existential. Ihde goes on to say, though, that Merleau-Ponty did not go far enough in that he did not take up the ways in which bodies are cultured and gendered. Ihde welcomes Foucault's ideas of the body as the "social body, the body politic, the malleable, disciplined body" (Ihde 2003, 12). However, he does not fully embrace Foucault's notions. Rather, he suggests that the body in the Merleau-Pontean sense need not be fully dissolved in the social, but that an embodied intentionality exists in which the body is lived through and is permeated by the social. This is one important place for intentionality to get posted.

For me, intentionality is the most important "old" phenomenological concept to preserve. As previously mentioned, I think it signifies interconnectedness, moves away from subjective knowing, and allows for consideration of a circulation of meanings. That is, I read intentionality a bit differently—a bit more post-structural perhaps—than many phenomenologists. Like Merleau-Ponty, I think the threads of intentionality connect all meaning that runs through relations. Perhaps unlike Merleau-Ponty, I think those threads are constantly being constructed, deconstructed, blurred, and disrupted. For me, intentionality is running all over the place, all the time—at times with clarity, but most often in the gnarliness of life.

So, when I "post" intentionality I am saying that intentionalities cannot be traced. One cannot start with the stable subject and try to follow that subject's intending toward and with the world. That very subject is both constructed and constructing, not dissolved. She is both agent and acted upon: what is available for that subject is both a manifestation of the social and is made possible by that subject's intending. This both/and move is important to a post-intentional conception as it complicates the subject just enough to keep the focus on the intentionalities, but does not fall prey to the view that all that circulates are intentionalities—that is, these intentionalities are brought into being by embodied subjects.

A second move that Ihde (2003) makes that is important for my purposes here is to simultaneously use and then post Husserl's idea of variation. Ihde stays true, so to speak, to Husserl's idea that the essence of any phenomenon has invariant and variant structures that make that phenomenon what it is. I like, though, how Ihde focuses almost solely on variants, for the most part discarding invariance and structure. He states,

> when multiple and complex "voices" are heard, no one voice is likely to emerge as singular. Second, when the voices are discordant, other patterns need to be sought.... And, to make one more point concerning the "voices" of evidence, harmonies are most likely to arise when there are convergences.... Postphenomenology is precisely the style of phenomenology which explicitly ... takes multidimensionality, multistability, and the multiple "voices" of things into account—to that degree it bears a family resemblance to the postmodern. (p. 24–25)

In this same way, a post-intentional phenomenology can do what old phenomenology could not—it can join the conversation about multiplicity, difference, and partiality. And I think this is important, for once we make this move it becomes more possible for post-intentional phenomenology itself to be a dialogic philosophy. One of the key ideas for me is that when old phenomenology stands alone it can only accomplish so much, and it seems stuck in-resistance-to Cartesian thinking while all sorts of other philosophies, post-structuralist ones in particular, have moved well past this concern. For me, post-structural conceptions of the way knowing and understanding are fleeting, momentary, tentative, and dangerous opens up phenomenology more—it draws out phenomenology not only as a philosophy of lived experience, but also as a philosophy capable of being used toward political ends.

How Post-Intentional Phenomenological Philosophy Can be Put to Use

Sokolowski (2000) has stated that "one of the great deficiencies of the phenomenological movement is its total lack of any political philosophy" (p. 226). To put an exclamation point on Sokolowski's claim, simple Google searches for political philosophers consistently identify names such as Plato, Socrates, Rawls, Marx, Gramsci, Dewey, Hegel, Rousseu, Foucault, and Derrida. Notably absent are Husserl, Heidegger, Sartre, Merleau-Ponty and Gadamer. Of course, this is not to say that phenomenological philosophers did not tend to important matters. Rather, their philosophizing is often not thought to be doing work on specific political and societal matters. I am not convinced that old phenomenology alone was designed , nor should it have been designed, to do political work. It was designed to do other important epistemological and ontological work.

Again, when Husserl introduced a phenomenological philosophy he was waging a philosophic, not necessarily a political, "on the ground" battle against centuries of Western philosophy and, in turn, social science that situated knowing and understanding either in minds or out in the world. The focus of these efforts and subsequent manifestations of phenomenology over the past century have been on this meaning connection, not on mobilizing this meaning connection for political purposes. In order to accomplish the latter, old phenomenology has needed to be put in conversation with other theories, and I think post-intentional phenomenology in particular is well poised to do so internally, so to speak. Why?

Post-Intentional Phenomenology as a Political Philosophy

Although old phenomenology alone has not been seen or used necessarily as a political philosophy, there are phenomenological craftspeople who have gone ahead and put phenomenology into play, or interplay, with more disruptive theories/methodologies. What I suggest in this part of the chapter is that even though Madeleine Grumet (1988)—renowned curriculum theorist who, in her powerful book *Bitter Milk: Women and Teaching*—characterized phenomenology alone as *assaulting and displacing the social sciences,* for me it is when she put phenomenology in dialogue with feminist theories that truly disruptive, political work could ensue. I see the same in Sara Ahmed's (2006) work, when she put queer theory in dialogue with phenomenology in articulating a queer phenomenology.

I begin my argument for post-intentional phenomenology as a political philosophy with Grumet and Ahmed not because they positioned their work as post-intentional, but because their work serves up excellent examples of the dialogic possibilities between phenomenology and other theories. I build upon Grumet and Ahmed's dialogism in order to establish the basis for the "internal" dialogism that exists within post-intentional phenomenology.

Grumet's Interplay between Feminism and Phenomenology

Throughout *Bitter Milk: Women and Teaching,* Grumet carefully weaves feminist theory and phenomenology together to create complicated images of women, mothering, and teaching. The powerful disruptions come through the interplay between her reading of phenomenological philosophers such as Merleau-Ponty and her complicating of gender and the way teaching and the work of women are positioned in a patriarchal society. Grumet's work initiates a discourse regarding gender and teaching that is powerful and pushes us to think differently. The political work is made possible through the interactions between phenomenological philosophy and feminism. Together, the two accomplish something really good that neither can accomplish in the same way on their own.

This is most evident when Grumet (1988) asserts "... if I designate the ground of my inquiry as the life world, you can imagine what you're left to work with" (p. 61). Nearly every word in this sentence is disruptive. I will slow down and open up a few here. First, "designating the ground of my inquiry" signals to readers that this is in fact what we are to do when we do our work. We must designate, not define or articulate. We must be specific about the ground of our inquiry. It might have been just fine for Grumet to use the broad moniker phenomenology, or perhaps a particular philosopher's conception of phenomenology. Instead, Grumet chooses a particular philosophical concept in phenomenology, the lifeworld. The lifeworld, again, is the intentional world, where meanings come into being—the interconnected space that Descartes had severed. In other words, Grumet chose a phenomenological term that pointed at the core of the radical philosophy Husserl wanted so much to become the science of all sciences. Her final phrase in this sentence, however, is the most powerful—"imagine what you're left to work with." I think there is more than one way to read this phrase.

One reading could be fairly quick and straightforward—you are left with nothing. Once you designate the ground of your inquiry as the lifeworld, there is literally nothing outside of these grounds to attend to, and that also means your task is infinite. Every single thing that comes into being as you move through your inquiry is important. Everything you intend phenomenologically is now part of your inquiry.

Another reading could lead you to focus on how the lifeworld, according to Grumet, actually "displaces the very world that social science addresses" (p. 61). What you are left with is a now-displaced world that has been, and continues to be, constructed by all sorts of forces—social science methodologies being one of them. More importantly, here is the opening for political work. When Grumet designates and demarcates the lifeworld from the world that the social sciences construct through methods and techniques, she creates openings for others to see how that world is not the same as the lifeworld. Her work exposes the masculinized hegemonic forces that provide a protective teflon coating over the lifeworld experiences, in Grumet's case, of women and the teaching that becomes feminized beneath the patriarchal structure. How Grumet sets up phenomenology and feminism opens up wounds. It brings both phenomenology and feminist thinking to bear on the matter of teaching. It draws out opportunities for phenomenological resonance with lived experiences and serves as a catalyst for feminist political possibilities.

Ahmed's Interplay between Queer Theory and Phenomenology

Another powerful example is Ahmed's (2006) *Queer Phenomenology: Orientations, Objects, Others.* Here, Ahmed does a marvelous job considering what it means "for sexuality to be lived as oriented" (p. 1). This deceptively simple, straightforward prepositional phrase contains some important disruptive nuances. For example, the phrase "lived as" brings, as with Grumet (1988), the lifeworld to the fore and reminds us that sexuality and orientation are brought into being in a directed, intentional manner (Husserl) and are embodied in and over time (Merleau-Ponty). Ahmed does not use abstractions to "define" sexuality and orientation. Rather, she carefully uses Husserl and Merleau-Ponty to bring sexuality, bodies, and orientation into being for readers—putting us in lived contact with objects and places as these objects and places become sexually oriented. In turn, Ahmed uses queer theory to extend phenomenology in important, disruptive ways, by not accepting the taken-for-granted assumptions regarding sexuality and orientation and therefore creating new ways of seeing spaces and places as oriented. Phenomenology becomes an agent, rather than the end. The larger purpose is not to do phenomenology for the sake of phenomenology alone, but to wield it for particular, political purposes.

I think seeing phenomenology as both a foundational philosophy and as an agent is a really important move that can and should be made. Ahmed does this quite beautifully in her book. She thoughtfully sets up a phenomenological conception of the body using philosophy and then does philosophical work to slow down and contemplate sexual orientation, not as a category or conception, but as ways of living and being in the world. Ahmed is not trying to test, construct, or build upon a queer theory of sexual orientation. Rather, she is trying to ground the matters of sexuality and orientation in the living of them. I think Husserl would appreciate how she is going to the "things themselves" and not trying to abstract or characterize them. I hope that queer theorists appreciate how Ahmed is able to open up how sexuality is lived as oriented.

Post-Intentionality's Internal Dialogism

When I say "internal" dialogism, I am suggesting that as a philosophy, post-intentional phenomenology is dialogic from the start. That is, unlike old phenomenology (an epistemological/ontological project) that requires "on the ground" theories to be put in dialogue with it, post-intentional phenomenology is conceptualized as traversing ontological and "on the ground" boundaries. This by no means suggests that post-intentional phenomenology does not benefit greatly from the same "external" dialogic moves Grumet and Ahmed made. Rather, here I articulate how post-intentionality is more dialogic than old phenomenology from the start, therefore making external dialogues with other philosophies/theories even more fertile and fruitful.

To demonstrate, I go to Deleuze and Guattari's (1987) conception of "lines of flight." In my ongoing development of a post-intentional phenomenology, I have found it increasingly necessary to emphasize the poststructural aspects. Deleuze and Guattari's lines of flight conception is particularly useful as it can help us see philosophically-oriented work as generative, creative, and complicated. In order to put their conception to work, it is important to make some sense of this concept.[3]

First, it is important to emphasize that a Deleuzo-Guattarian vocabulary privileges how things connect rather than what things are (Lorraine 2005). As such, the concept, lines of flight, does not assume that any thing, idea, belief, goal, phenomenon, person, animal, object, etc. can be thought of as stable, singular, and final. Instead, all things are connected and interconnected in all sorts of unstable, changing, partial, fleeting ways. This is important to post-intentional phenomenology as a political philosophy as the connective nature of social, ethical, and political relations does not lend itself to simplicities and essences. It does lend itself to complexities and tentative understandings.

So, Deleuze and Guatarri's insights offer post-intentional phenomenological craftspeople with "innovative ways to conceptualize *things* as fluid, shape-shifting assemblages continually on the move in interacting with the world, rather than perceiving them as stable essences" (Vagle and Hofsess 2014, p.1). Putting lines of flight to work, as a philosophical construction, serves as a way to discuss and open up complicated movements and interactions, as well as a means to explore how these assemblages encounter the work of post-intentional phenomenological craftwork.

Next, it is important to understand that for Deleuze and Guatarri (1987), lines of flight are one of three kinds of lines, perhaps the most radical, and perhaps the most difficult to identify and sustain. They discuss "molar lines"—the rigid space characterized by binaries, "molecular lines" where subtle cracks in the rigid lines occur allowing for more fluidity but are always in danger of being sucked back into the rigid, and "lines of flight", that no longer tolerate the rigid and explode beyond it. Post-intentional phenomenology assumes that phenomena, too, are always already exploding through relations, and that the post-intentional phenomenologist's primary job is to not shy away from these potential explosions.

When enacting post-intentional phenomenology, it is critical that one resists binaries such as either-or thinking, right-wrong, normal-abnormal, and the rigidity that often continues after a binary begins to break down. Rigid thinking can lead to rigid decision-making, rigid perceptivity, and rigid methodologies. I am not suggesting that one does not need to make decisions when doing politically-oriented research. One will need to take a stand and proceed. However, the idea expressed here concerning the practice of a post-intentional phenomenological philosophy is to remain open, flexible, and contemplative in our thinking, acting, and decision-making.

A third important, and related, thing to understand is that lines of flight can be conceived as resisting the tying down of lived experience and knowledge. Although I do not believe old phenomenology intended to tie down phenomena, the adherence to essence communicates, or at least is interpreted as communicating, the opposite. The concept of lines of flight can help us think differently in phenomenology about lived experiences and knowledge. It assumes that knowledge takes "off" in ways that we may not be able to anticipate. Post-intentional phenomenological craftspeople are encouraged, then, to follow these lines of flight—realizing that any time we follow a line of flight in our research we run the risk of being pulled back into rigid, either-or thinking. In old phenomenology, the goal was to determine the essential structure a phenomenon "has." In post-intentional phenomenology the goal is to see what the phenomenon might become.

Finally and most importantly, although most if not all of us, realistically, spend our energies working along and through the molar (e.g., my theoretical frame allows me to say this, but does not allow me to say that) and molecular lines (e.g., my arguments can be deeply contextual and situational, yet are still limited to a set of options determined by other powers, knowledges, structures), we are encouraged to make every effort to identify and boldly follow possible lines of flight toward something either not-yet-discovered or unknown. Sometimes these lines of flight might be perceived as big and radical, and other times, more subtle. Whatever the case, the lines of flight always aim to flee the tight boundaries of any theoretical framework and method, understanding that these lines of flight will not remove us from the pull to rigidity and structure—rather we will find ourselves in constant tensions as the flights proceed.

Making Post-Intentional Philosophy Concrete and Actionable

I close this chapter with another phenomenological encounter. My purpose is to make what I have described here actionable on the philosophical level, so that we are well positioned to do the same on the methodological level. With this in mind, I share the course description from a doctoral seminar I have taught entitled, *Phenomenological Philosophies and Pedagogy,* framed by similar arguments I have made in this chapter. Although the course did not focus specifically on post-intentional phenomenology, this description does provide a heuristic for how one might begin, especially in doctoral education, to live out the dialogic commitments between phenomenology and other theories emphasized in this chapter, and then how one might perhaps proceed to the post-intentional.

Phenomenological Encounter #15
Becoming Philosophically Dialogic

Course Description

Recently, I have asserted three reasons why phenomenology can be read as a particularly powerful way of philosophizing: 1) it counters centuries of Western philosophy; 2) it provides an apparatus—intentionality—for this countering; and 3) it moves social sciences away from "knowing concerns" (epistemology) and toward "being concerns" (ontology).

The first purpose of this doctoral seminar is to **spend time together as scholars trying to figure out what in the world this means and why it matters**. We will read some phenomenological philosophy (e.g., Husserl, Merleau-Ponty, Sartre, Heidegger, Gadamer) and some work from contemporary philosophers who work to make sense of phenomenology (e.g., Sokolowski, Moran and Mooney).

We will then survey all sorts of conceptions of pedagogy (e.g., critical, psychological, feminist, culturally-relevant, sociological, queer, developmental, pragmatic, social-constructivist) in order **to create a landscape for how pedagogy has been imagined**.

Finally, each of us will choose a particular aspect of phenomenological philosophy and a particular conception of pedagogy in order to (as Sara Ahmed [2006] does with phenomenological philosophy and queer theory) "put them in closer dialogue" with one another. **In doing so, we will each put our philosophical and theoretical dialogues to use on a nagging pedagogical (and practical) issue, concern, or problem we care about.**

Some students decided to work with theories of gender and race, others with theories of social class and compassion, particularly coming from Buddhism. In all cases, these scholars, some now on faculty at universities around the United States, found unique and important ways to put what might seem to be competing discourses in dialogue. For example, they put phenomenology (perceived as an "a-political" philosophy) and theoretical conceptions of pedagogy into closer dialogue with one another in order to try to address something important on the ground. The goal was to perhaps help phenomenology reclaim some of its radical roots and, more importantly, to live out Grumet's (1988) view that phenomenology itself serves as an assaulting displacement of the social sciences. We now consider the methodological ways in which this work can be carried out post-intentionally.

CHAPTER EIGHT

Post-Intentional Methodology

In some of my earlier work, I introduced a post-intentional phenomeno-logical research approach (Vagle 2010a) in an effort to reframe Donald Schon's call for a phenomenology of practice.[1] In this chapter, I draw on and extend my initial efforts in order to further articulate a post-intentional phenomenological research approach that can be used by those interested in crafting such research and more generally as a resource for all qualitative researchers as they mentor others interested in crafting post-intentional phenomenological research. To this end, I have written this chapter as a resource that qualitative researchers can use to design post-intentional phenomenological research.

I articulate my five-component approach based on the philosophical underpinnings I discussed in chapter 7, as well as the philosophical ideas related to through-ness–oriented phenomenological research. This chapter is written as a guide, and therefore the tone of the writing shifts from more traditional academic writing to a practical "here's what you do" description. I continue to use phenomenological encounters in order to provide concrete examples of what various aspects of the approach might look and feel like.

In order to create the methodological process for post-intentional phenomenology I put in dialogue particular aspects of my understanding of van Manen's and Dahlberg, Dahlberg, and Nystrom's approaches; Hei-degger's notion of manifestations; my interpretations of the philosophical notion of intentionality; and post-structural commitments to knowledge always, already being tentative and never complete. What resulted is a five-component process for conducting post-intentional phenomenologi-cal research.

1. Identify a phenomenon in its multiple, partial, and varied contexts.
2. Devise a clear, yet flexible process for gathering data appropriate for the phenomenon under investigation.
3. Make a post-reflexion plan.
4. Read and write your way through your data in a systematic, responsive manner.
5. Craft a text that captures tentative manifestations of the phenomenon in its multiple, partial, and varied contexts.

As I have stressed throughout this book, I remain in full agreement with van Manen and Dahlberg in stating that phenomenological research components should not be viewed in a linear "methods" fashion, but in an open and shifting cyclical pattern. This means that you will need to continually revisit all five components throughout the research process. I also want to stress that although my five-component process is designed as a cohesive whole, I think it is equally possible to pick and choose elements of the design that work well for you and leave out elements that do not work quite as well. That is, I want the post-structural commitment to all knowing being multiple, fleeting, and partial to also apply to my design process.

Research Component #1: Identify a Phenomenon in its Multiple, Partial, and Varied Contexts

Although we have spent considerable time throughout the book discussing what a phenomenon is to phenomenologists, I think it serves us well to be reminded of two key points. Again, phenomenological researchers study phenomena—Heidegger (1998[1927]) says these can be understood as "that which becomes manifest for us." Dahlberg, Drew, and Nystrom (2001) add that a phenomenon is any thing or part of the world "as it presents itself to, or, as it is experienced by, a subject" (p. 45). And phenomena appear in our intentional relationships with others and things in the lifeworld. It is the particular ways in which *we* find ourselves in the world that we are trying to identify, and in turn study.

In order to identify a phenomenon in this manner of speaking, I think it is important to systematically state the research problem, complete a partial review of the literature, make a philosophical claim relative to the research problem, articulate the phenomenon and the accompanying research questions, situate the phenomenon in the multiple, partial, and varied contexts in which it tends to manifest, and select the research participants.

State the Research Problem

State the large, overarching concern empirically, theoretically, personally and practically for you as a scholar. Be sure to answer the question: Why is this important to study? If you are proposing a thesis or dissertation study, your advisor and committee may want a fairly substantive statement of the research problem. Unless this is the case for you, I would encourage something concise—two to three pages. This is especially important if you are proposing research to funding agencies or award committees. You will not have much space, so get to your main and most important point in the first few sentences. Here is an example I recently crafted based on a larger project I co-created and co-direct with Dr. Stephanie Jones.

Phenomenological Encounter #16
Statement of the Research Problem

"When I grow up I want to be a waitress just like my mom." (A Little Girl)
"Oh, you can do so much *better* than that!" (Her Teacher)

Children articulating aspirations for working-class futures are likely to hear responses similar to the one here, one that my colleague, Dr. Stephanie Jones (University of Georgia), and I heard from a teacher during one of our professional development workshops entitled "The Other Side of Poverty in Schools." Such a response is informed by neoliberal discourses of social class and the assumed purposes of schooling: upward mobility in status, income, and perceived contribution to national economic growth is the goal and anything else is a disappointment (e.g. Aronowitz 2008; Rose 1989). The "social class ladder" metaphor aligns, then, with the idea that those on the bottom rungs earn less in wages, status, and overall perceived value and therefore, in order to be recognized as valuable to society either through measures of salary or prestige, must work relentlessly to climb the ladder.

Although "climbing the ladder" is often interpreted as an unquestioned goal, this sort of upward mobility discourse constructs classist hierarchies in schools and classroom practice and is founded on misconceptions of work (e.g. Crawford 2011; Rose 2005), lived experiences of social class (e.g. Reay 2004/2005), and the broader social and economic context of the United States and the world (e.g. Berliner 2006; Faux 2012). Educators engaging upward mobility discourses without doing the work it takes to better understand what is informing those discourses—and the economic policies shaping workers' realities—may unwittingly alienate the very students they hope to inspire.

This problem adversely affects student performance in classrooms as well, as social class remains the best predictor of educational engagement and achievement (e.g. Berliner 2005; Rothstein 2004) and the nation's income achievement gap between rich and poor children is the widest it has been in the past fifty years (Reardon 2011). In an effort to begin to address this pervasive problem, I collaborated with Dr. Jones to co-found (in 2010) and co-direct The CLASSroom Project—a dynamic project aimed at making all classrooms places where children and families are not advantaged or disadvantaged as a result of social class background.

One of the initiatives I have led as part of The CLASSroom Project, "Social Class-Sensitive Photo-Storying," began spring 2012 as a professional developmental experience designed to help elementary teachers at Maple Leaf Elementary School (pseudonym) gain a deeper understanding of their students' lives—especially students from working-class and poor backgrounds who don't typically "see" themselves in the stories, assignments, and assessments they experience at school. During the 2013-14 academic year, we would like to study how photo-storying is experienced in these classrooms. In short, photo-storying, drawing on photo-elicitation pedagogical practices (e.g, Marquez-Zenkov 2007), asks teachers and youth to take pictures of important aspects of their lives, work, and play, and use those pictures to dignify the lived experiences of all children, cultivate deeper understandings, and make meaningful connections with one another in the classroom.

Partial Review of the Literature

Situate your research problem in existing scholarly conversations in clearly articulated field(s), but do not spend extensive time reviewing literature before conducting the study. I articulated my rationale for this in chapter 5, so I will not go into great depth here other than to briefly highlight a few points. Although partial reviews of the literature run counter to conventional norms, it is important to remember that the primary goal in post-intentional phenomenology is to capture tentative manifestations of the phenomenon as it is lived—not use existing theories to explain or predict what might take place. So, situate the phenomenon, but do not spend a lot of time building a "literature case." However, you can and should bring literature in the field to bear as fully as possible when you craft your text (see component #5).

Philosophical Claim

Make entry into at least one philosophical conversation in phenomenology. I think this is quite important, given phenomenology's strong philosophical roots and given that all high-amplitude phenomenologists have designed their approaches with a strong philosophical base. I, as articulated throughout this book and in chapter 7 in particular, have followed suit in my philosophizing of post-intentionality. In order to craft post-intentional phenomenological research, I think it is important to do the same.

Philosophical claims can take many forms. Oftentimes, when designing a study, philosophical claims can start with one philosophical idea from one philosopher, and then they might grow throughout a study. Other times, you might decide to dig into a few ideas from one philosopher. And at yet other times, it might feel better to work across a number of philosophers in order to portray the landscape of phenomenological philosophy, such as in the example below. I encourage openness and creativity here. Do not limit yourself. And most importantly, in post-intentional phenomenology, it is important to remember that we treat all knowledge and all philosophical ideas as partial, fleeting, malleable, and ever-changing. If Husserl helps you, use him. If he does not, do not. If putting Merleau-Ponty's thoughts on embodiment in dialogue with Sartre's thoughts on emotion helps you, then put them in dialogue with one another.

The key thing to remember with this particular sub-component is that to do phenomenological research one must know the philosophy. In many respects, phenomenological philosophy and phenomenological human science research are delicately intertwined, crossing lines between philosophical and empirical work. Again, I have not read a leading high-amplitude phenomenological researcher who did not have a deep understanding of the philosophy and who did not use it consistently in his or her work. Do this by writing a clear, concise description of the philosophy—a couple paragraphs will suffice when writing the initial proposal. You will expand upon this description as you craft your text (see component #5). Here is the first paragraph of Dr. Joseph Pate's (2012) philosophical claim.

Phenomenological Encounter #17
A Philosophical Claim

Phenomenology is first and foremost a philosophy (Moran 2002; Sokolowski 2000). As with any philosophical approach (Christian 1994), phenomenology is grounded in and informed by core tenets and assumptions as it addresses broader and more metaphysical questions and assertions. Phenomenology, however, is also a research methodology (Butler-Kisber 2010; Creswell 2007; Crotty 2003) offering an organizing strategy for researching lived-experiences (van Manen 2001). A commitment to phenomenological research insists competence of methods to equal parts philosophical exploration, scholarship, and understanding (Vagle 2010a). At its core, phenomenology is a disruptive and critical approach to our lived-experiences aimed at illuminating our intentional relationships with the world around us and how phenomenon are manifested for/to us (Heidegger 1998[1927]; Vagle 2010a). Posited as an ontological and epistemological orientation (Dahlberg, Dahlberg, and Nystrom 2008; Heidegger, 2002a, 2002b, 2002c; Vagle, 2010a), phenomenology attempts to "get behind" our taken-for-granted perspectives of lived experiences to reveal glimpses, both tentative and fleeting, of phenomenon as they are lived, not theorized.

Statement of Phenomenon (Research Question[s])

Describe the phenomenon through what I call an "intentionality statement." An intentionality statement is a clear and direct statement of the phenomenon under investigation. It explicitly identifies your understanding of intentionality philosophically and concludes with the identification of the phenomenon—that is, something related to humans' intentional relationship with the world. Close this section by writing a primary phenomenological research question that begins with either "What is it like to ...", "What does it mean to ...", or "What is it to find oneself ...". Craft one to three secondary research questions that help you focus your data collection plan toward the primary phenomenological research question.

When I first started crafting phenomenological research, I did not concern myself with secondary research questions. However, as I have served on doctoral committees and received feedback from funding agencies, I have noticed that those outside of phenomenological research often ask for more detail and specification regarding the research question. For many, the broad nature of the primary research question feels a bit too philosophical. So, I have found it necessary to articulate secondary research questions that can inform some of the specific data-gathering and analysis methods later in the study. Here are some excerpts from Ms. Keri Valentine's statement of the phenomenon, including her intentionality statement and research questions.

Phenomenological Encounter #18
An Intentionality Statement

Although the aims and methods of these phenomenologies transform over time, a commitment to investigating intentionality remains central. In phenomenology, intentionality is where one looks to find meaning. This "where" isn't a place one can point to—it doesn't merely reside within people and things. Intentionality is more to do with the relations running through the lifeworld, and probably is most analogous to the traditional Chinese ch'i, or life force. This is the reason phenomenology investigates intentionalities of human experience—the experience that Husserl demonstrates even allows science to mathematize the world. "To the things themselves" means getting to these relationships between humans and the world....

Vagle identifies three roots of post-intentional phenomenological research: "Heidegger's manifestations, the philosophical notion of intentionality, and post-structural commitments to knowledge always, already being tentative and never complete" (Vagle 2010b, 6). These all affect how Vagle (2010b) comes to describe intentionality, which is:

> Whatever understanding is opened up through an investigation will always move with and through the researcher's intentional relationships with the phenomena—not simply in the researcher, in the participants, in the text, or in their power positions, but in the dynamic intentional relationships that tie participants, the researcher, the produced text, and their positionality together. In this way, intentionality is always moving, is unstable and therefore can be read post-structurally. (p. 5)

Phenomenon. This investigation does not attempt to look at the whole of perception/perspective, but rather examines perspective taking and perspective creating of the visual domain. Perspective is a constant current running through much of human action (and probably non-human)—reacting to an emotionally moving book, engaging conversation, etc.... The phenomena of interest in this study aims to articulate the lived quality of perceiving space that is problematized through tools and events that mediate one's perception....

Research questions.... The primary question concerns the learners' experience and asks what is it for students to find themselves perceiving space as mediated in a variety of ways through technology? Secondary questions help further focus the work and seek to inform future iterations of the design. These include: (1) What role does the learning environment play in the experience for students? (2) What is the experience of mathematizing reality? (3) How do the various forms of communication (Skype, face-to-face, blogs, photo diary, etc.) unfold and what is the affect of this on their experience? (4) How does the experience seem to change over the course of the design?

Contexts

Situate the phenomenon in the multiple and varied contexts in which you believe it resides; keep in mind that this decision will guide your data-gathering and analysis plan and also serve as merely a starting point. You will need to remain open to the phenomenon as you are studying it. This means that you will need to make analytic decisions about going to new contexts if the phenomenon appears to come to be in these new contexts. You will not know until you get there. You also must "persistently critique" (St. Pierre 1997) your own knowing, as your understanding of the phenomenon is a set of performances within your relationship with the phenomenon.

This part of the methodological design can be unnerving, especially for those who want to know exactly where the study will reside. I do understand there are limits to the contexts in which we study. We have to make choices. In this sub-component I am encouraging you to think carefully about the contexts and micro-contexts in which phenomenon shift and change. So I mean context in the broad sense of the term and context in the more specified sense of thinking about spaces, places, embodiments, situations, and moments, all of which are partial and fleeting. We return again to Keri Valentine's work in order to capture a glimpse of how she contextualized her study.

Phenomenological Encounter #19
Contexts Where the Phenomenon Resides

The phenomenon of a changing spatial perspective most likely inhabits all humans (and even animals), not only in places, but also across time. The simple motion of stepping a foot to the side necessarily changes one's perspective—their distance and point of view in relation to objects shift. As humans age, they grow taller and relate to the world differently. The perspective of a chair and even the way one sits down changes over time. It seems that every moment is a change in perspective, even if it is mostly unconscious and not reflected upon. This leads to a focus on contexts in which humans' perspective shifts suddenly, or can at least be compared to an earlier, different perspective.

Non-seeing perspectives. Although it is impossible to consider all the lifeworld in this one investigation, I believe the phenomenon of changed perspective resides everywhere. Non-seeing perspectives, such as those in literature and conversations, are likely contributing events that change one's future visual perspective. The nature of being a body in space that interacts with others, things, and ideas inevitably means perspective (whether in a natural or phenomenological attitude) is always circulating through everything.

Multiplicity. After reading Ihde's (1993) chapter on literate and illiterate cultures and their art, I was struck by the images of art from differing perspectives that seemed related to a perspective one might take when reading a book (angled, slightly from the sky) or an undefined perspective (in aboriginal, non-literate cultures). Egyptian art seemed to show multiple perspectives in one painting, similar to cubist modern art that endeavors to capture multiple moments of time (girl walking down a staircase) or Picasso's faces (multiple perspectives of the nose). Being embodied in the world does not allow us to take on multiple perspectives simultaneously, but paintings, multiple-exposure photographs, film, and other technologies do. Humans do of course have two eyes that create a sense of depth, so perhaps there is a multiplicity of perspective on some level.

Participant Selection

Select research participants who have experienced the phenomenon under investigation, whom you think will be able to provide a thorough and rich description of the phenomenon, and who collectively represent the range of multiple, partial, and varied contexts that you have identified. I discussed this in some detail in chapter 5, so please reference that chapter for a reminder.

Research Component #2: Devise a Clear, Yet Flexible Process for Gathering Data Appropriate for the Phenomenon Under Investigation

In post-intentional phenomenology, like other phenomenological research approaches, researchers go to those who have experienced the phenomenon of interest through the use of common qualitative data-gathering techniques such as interviews, observations, and writings to describe/ interpret the phenomenon. At the same time, and as I emphasized in chapter 6, there are innumerable ways to gather data. So, I reiterate here the guiding principles of being open and creative about the data you choose to gather.

It is important to remember that one is not studying individual participants or the objects of their experience. Rather, one is studying one's participants' intentional relationship with the phenomenon under investigation. For instance, in another study I conducted (Vagle 2011) I aimed to learn more about what it is like for teachers and students to use formative assessment to prepare for the end-of-year high-stakes tests. Although I was interested in teachers, students, and the tests, neither the teachers, the students, nor the tests constituted the units of analyses. Rather, the units of analyses were the intentional relationships among the teachers, students, and the tests. I used Sartre's (in Moran and Mooney 2002) conception of intentionality as I studied how participanting teachers and students found themselves bursting forth toward the phenomenon (Vagle 2009) under investigation.

Again, you need to make decisions, but remain open in doing so. In post-intentional research, think broadly and creatively about what data is appropriate. If the phenomenon calls for numbers (i.e., frequencies, measures of central tendency), then include them. If the phenomenon calls for fictional writings, photo elicitation, or re-enactments of lived experiences, then include such data sources. Feel free to use data sources that might appear to "belong" to other research approaches. For instance, a trademark of ethnographic research is sustained fieldwork, often in the form of observations—use sustained fieldwork if it makes sense given the phenomenon.

Sometimes it is difficult to determine how you will gather data (e.g., what you will ask, what you will observe, for how long, in what contexts). As a general rule, plan to collect more data than you might need. Remain open to changes and adjustments you might need to make along the way. Also, slow down a bit and take the time to practice. It is often good to conduct a short pilot study in order to try out various data-gathering techniques.

Select Data Sources

Once you have selected your initial data sources, I think it is important to describe in one paragraph or so how you will gather data using each data source. Make a convincing case for how these data are essential (as in really important—not as in the essence of the phenomenon) for opening up this particular phenomenon in the multiple, partial, and varied contexts that you have identified. Here is another glimpse from Keri Valentine's study.

Phenomenological Encounter #20
Describing a Data Source

Lived-experience descriptions. After students (approximately thirty) have completed their investigation of space and perspective, they will be invited to generate a written lived-experience description about what it was like to perceive space during the investigations and the meaning of this experience in their lives. The description will be used during a follow-up interview to help students articulate their experiences more fully and/or clarify students' experiences. I will communicate with students by e-mail to request their lived-experience description. Van Manen's (2001) suggestions will be used, which include: asking participants to describe the investigation of space as they experienced it, avoiding "casual explanations, generalizations, and abstract interpretations," including "feelings, moods, and emotions," focusing on "particular examples," and choosing an example "which stands out for its vividness, or as it was the first time" (p. 27). The lived-experience description gives students an opportunity to reflect on particulars of the phenomenon without as much scaffolding as might occur in an interview. Not only does this serve as a springboard for later interviews but may open up aspects of the phenomenon not yet considered.

Align Data Sources with Research Questions

Although I continue to suggest that post-intentional craftspeople respond to this sub-component, I have received feedback from some that it feels a bit clumsy. I have kept it, though, primarily for practical reasons. Again, I have served on doctoral committees in which this has been requested of doctoral students and have received feedback on research proposals to funding agencies supporting this practice. And often, reviewers like lists and tables. I think the graphic shift in text helps readers, and provides something concrete within what usually is a dense discussion of philosophy, theory, and methodology. So, I encourage you to list each research question, primary and/or secondary, and then identify which data source(s) you will use to address each question. It might also be helpful to include information regarding number of (e.g., interviews or observations), in what contexts, and over what period of time. Although Ms. Angelica Pazurek's example below does not include all of these components, it nicely illustrates what I mean.

Primary Research Questions	Data Sources
Q1: What is it like to be an adult learner in online learning environments?	• Transcripts from audio-recorded individual interviews conducted with participants in person or via online web conferencing • Participants' written lived experience descriptions • Written, audio, and video artifacts shared by participants throughout the course on the online course website • Researcher's online bridling journal
Q2: What is it like to experience engagement in online learning environments?	• Transcripts from audio-recorded individual interviews conducted with participants in person or via online web conferencing • Participants' written lived experience descriptions • Written, audio, and video narrative artifacts shared by participants throughout the course on the online course website • Researcher's online bridling journal
Q3: How do various elements of learning online and dynamics of the learning environment influence adult learners' feelings of engagement?	• Transcripts from audio-recorded individual interviews conducted with participants in person or via online web conferencing • Participants' written lived experience descriptions • Written, audio, and video narrative artifacts shared by participants throughout the course on the online course website • Researcher's online bridling journal

Research Component #3: Make a *Post-Reflexion* Plan

Although it is difficult to pin down the most important component of the post-intentional approach, if forced to do so I would choose this one. As discussed at length earlier in this book, bridling requires us to stretch our idea of openness and humility, and this stretching is a necessary part of this type of research. In post-intentional phenomenological research it is important to go further with our reflexivity,[2] however. Although Dahlberg's (2006) bridling metaphor (i.e., tightening and loosening the intentional threads [reins] that tie us meaningfully to the world) gets closer to the active, persistent reflexivity—looking at what we usually look through—that I think is important, some commitments in post-structural philosophies are necessary in order to realize a deeply layered, complex, and nuanced (post)reflexivity.

Scholars (e.g., Davies and Gannon 2006; Lather, 1993) who theorize qualitative research methodologies often describe reflexivity in terms of how researchers can learn to pay careful attention to the complex socially-constructed ways in which reality gets framed through our researching and writing as a qualitative researcher. They stress that what we assert is always already framed in ways of which we may not be aware. Again, Lather writes: "It is not a matter of looking harder or more closely, but of seeing what frames our seeing-spaces of constructed visibility and incitements to see which constitute power/knowledge" (p. 675).

In order to make "trying to see what frames our seeing" (Lather 1993) less abstract in our crafting of post-intentional phenomenological research, I have found it helpful to employ four strategies that my colleague, Stephanie Jones, and I use in our work with practicing educators. As post-intentional phenomenological craftswomen and men, it is important to pay attention to:

1. Moments when they/we instinctively **connect** with what they/we observe and moments in which they/we instinctively **disconnect**.
2. Our **assumptions of normality.**
3. Our **bottom lines,** that is those beliefs, perceptions, perspectives, opinions that we refuse to shed; and
4. Moments in which they/we are **shocked** by what they/we observe.

These sorts of self-reflexive commitments hold promise in creating a more radical reflexivity that can begin to uncover underlying, shifting, changing knowledges that are at work in all intentional relations, and can begin to embrace post-structural arguments such as all knowing being partial and fleeting.

As we post-reflex through a study it is important to document, wonder about and question our connections/discussions, assumptions of what we take to be normal, bottom lines, and moments we are shocked. For it is in these moments that our post-reflexive work needs to take place, and this means we must constantly interrogate our pre-understandings and developing understandings of the phenomenon. This is important, as one does not want to have the crafted text become an autobiographical account in its entirety.

At the same time, a post-intentional approach acknowledges and welcomes the fact that, as researchers, all of our work is in part autobiographical. In writing about some of Gadamer's influence on phenomenological research, Dahlberg, Dahlberg, and Nystrom (2008) remind us that we must understand ourselves as historical beings who are always tethered to the past. We cannot escape being parts of history and can never re-position ourselves outside of tradition and history. So, crafting a post-intentional, post-reflexive text also presses us to question our understandings, the traditions we are operating within, and the history we are launching from—while carefully examining the participants' experiences. From a practical standpoint, here are three things I suggest you do as you practice post-reflexivity in your crafting:

Create a Post-Reflexion Journal

From a technical standpoint, start writing in a journal early and write in it often—as soon as you begin to craft your research proposal. Use it as a space to wonder, question, think, contradict yourself, agree with yourself, vent, scream, laugh, and celebrate. There are many ways to do this. I have seen people hand-write in a notebook, word-process in a single ongoing document, blog, use tumblr (e.g., Pazurek's phenomenology runs), use an audio recorder, video-blog. Whatever form you use, be sure to date each entry. This will not only help you put your thinking in a temporal sequence, but will be useful when you draw on some of your self-reflexive thoughts when you craft your text.

Write an "Initial Post-Reflexion Statement"

Very early in your research process, sometime soon after you have identified the phenomenon, write an "initial post-reflexion statement." This is similar to "subjectivity statements" that are often used in qualitative research. However, I see this a bit differently. Like subjectivity statements, it is important to describe your role as a researcher, your assumptions, beliefs, and perspectives, and your background—especially as all of these relate to the phenomenon. In a post-reflexion statement, though, I think it is important to see this statement as merely the beginning of an ongoing process of post-reflexing. Sometimes, subjectivity statements appear to be once and for all, and are not revisited throughout the research process. In post-intentional phenomenological research it is important to continue to revisit, throughout the study, what you write in this statement.

It is also important to have your initial statements not only focus on your personal beliefs and perspectives, but also what frames your perspectives, beliefs, and perceptions. In your statement, begin to try to see what frames your seeing—that is, your connections/disconnections, assumptions of normality, bottom lines, and what shocks you. Say what you think you will learn from your participants. Although some might feel this will limit your openness, I argue the opposite point. Examining your own assumptions gives you a better chance of taking hold of them, rather than the assumptions taking hold of you and in turn the phenomenon under investigation. Again, revisit this statement throughout data gathering and analysis and write new statements regularly.

Post-Reflex as You Gather and Analyze Data

Finally, I think it is helpful to create and describe a system for writing in your journal, whatever form it takes. For example, it might be good to write an entry after each data gathering event. Be sure to date each entry and always think about your journaling as a data source for the crafting of your text.

Research Component #4: Read and Write Your Way through Your Data in a Systematic, Responsive Manner.

This research activity constitutes the heart of data analysis. As I stated in chapter 6, most high-amplitude phenomenological researchers advocate for a whole-parts-whole analysis process and the same holds with a post-intentional approach. Please refer to that portion of chapter 6 for technical guidance, and then return here for an important extension of whole-part-whole analyses, namely, how we can make the transition from the analytic "wholes" that result from your whole-part-whole analysis toward tentative manifestations of the phenomenon.

This is a very important part of the analysis process, for it is at this point that the text you are going to craft clearly becomes post-intentional. That is, once you have "wholes" it is now time to deconstruct these wholes. I give pause here, as this most likely will seem counterintuitive. After all, why go through a whole-part-whole analysis only to take these wholes apart? Here are two concrete reasons:

1. I have found that the best way to find tentative manifestations is to first get a strong sense of what might "mark" the phenomenon. So, I continue to follow, generally speaking, what other approaches do with analysis (e.g., Giorgi and his pursuit of invariant structures, van Manen and his pursuit of essential themes) because I do think going through the analytic process of whole-part-whole forces us to dig deeply into and across our data. And this digging gives us opportunities to better see the shifting, fleeting, and fluid nature of phenomena. That brings me to a second reason.
2. I have found that it is best to have something(s) concrete to work with at this stage. I am a bit uneasy if craftspeople dive into data from the start saying, "I am now looking for tentative manifestations of the phenomenon." Although the fifth and final component of a post-intentional research approach explicitly focuses on crafting a text that captures the tentative manifestations of the phenomenon, I think in order for this to be accomplished we must have done the hard work of getting to tentative manifestations. And this hard work comes during analysis when we read and write through the data in a systematic manner.

What then do we do when we deconstruct the wholes? The most useful way to carry out this part of the process is to operationalize Deleuze and

Guattari's (1987) philosophical idea—lines of flight. In the following phenomenological encounter I briefly review the philosophical basis for using this concept that I more fully described in chapter 7, and then articulate how it can be used as the final part of a post-intentional analysis protocol.[3]

Phenomenological Encounter #21
Post-Intentional Data Analysis as Chasing Lines of Flight

In order to put this philosophical conception to use methodologically, I suggest two analytic "noticings:"

Noticing #1: Actively Look for Ways that Knowledge "Takes Off".

Lines of Flight resist the tying down of lived experience and knowledge. It assumes that knowledge takes "off" in ways that we may not be able to anticipate. So, it is important to carefully and persistently look at our whole-part-whole analysis and our own post-reflexive journaling and ask ourselves questions such as: **What doesn't seem to fit? If I follow this "mis-fit" notion, idea, insight, perspective, what might I learn about the phenomenon that is not yet think-able?**

I think it is very important at this final stage of analysis to pay attention to how our bodies and emotions respond to these sorts of questions. Hofsess (2013), in her study, discussed her "embodied intensities" during data gathering and analysis. I think noticing and writing through and about our embodied intensities gives us the opportunity to notice the ways phenomenological manifestations are center fleeing rather than center seeking. However, we only can communicate what we notice in this regard if we actively look for explosions of thought.

Noticing #2: Distinguish Lines of Flight from Other Lines Operating on Us and the Phenomenon

As described in chapter 7, lines of flight are, arguably, the third, perhaps most radical, and perhaps most difficult to identify and sustain. Post-intentional phenomenology assumes that phenomena, too, are always, already exploding through relations, and that the post-intentional phenomenologist's primary job is to write our way through these explosions. In order to distinguish lines of flight with molar and molecular lines, pose the following questions of your readings of the data:

1. **Where might I have retreated to either/or thinking?** *Try to break up these binaries by posing alternative ways of thinking.*
2. **Where might I appear "certain" of what something means?** *In these cases, ask yourself why such certainty? And then challenge yourself to see the uncertainties.*
3. **Where might I have extended to something creative and intriguing, but then backed off to something a bit more**

safe? *This is particularly important. Don't be afraid to take risks. Identify moments where you began to take a risk but then retreated to something more "rational" and "explanatory". Once you have identified a moment such as this, challenge yourself to wonder, create, explode in your thinking of what is at play.*

4. **Where might I appear "uncertain" of what something means?** *I think these can be some of the most exciting and hopeful sites for line of flight explosions. When you return to your data and locate sites of uncertainty, these are the spaces where you are most likely to find something incomprehensible about the phenomenon. Do not back away from these uncertainties—for they are the richest space for explosive insights, a true opening up of what the phenomenon under investigation might become.*

Research Component #5: Craft a Text that Captures Tentative Manifestations of the Phenomenon in its Multiple, Partial, and Varied Contexts

For van Manen (2001), the phenomenon becomes animated and meaningful to others through the careful crafting of a phenomenological description. These types of descriptions aim "to transform lived experience into a textual expression of its essence—in such a way that the effect of the text is at once a reflexive re-living and a reflective appropriation of something meaningful" (p. 36). Although van Manen directly references essence, his phrase "transform lived experience into a textual expression" resonates with my post-intentional approach.

This work is particularly challenging as it requires much more than listing the tentative manifestations and cannot be adequately articulated in a step-by-step manner. As van Manen aptly describes it, this research activity is an art. Consistent with this theme's book, this is the culminating moment in which we craft. Although I think it is helpful to read a number of phenomenological descriptions across phenomenological approaches to get a sense of the tone and quality of the writing, I think it is even more important to think outside of traditional form and go to examples that explode beyond tradition.

In chapter 9, I provide highlights from some post-intentional phenomenological studies. Before I do so, however, here are some things to think about as you begin to make decisions about crafting your post-intentional phenomenological text.

1. Re-State the Multiple and Varied Contexts.

This can and should be brief. The important point is to remind yourself that the text needs to reflect these contexts. These are almost guaranteed to change, but with a post-intentional approach, be in the habit of thinking contextually while you are writing phenomenologically.

2. *Brainstorm Potential Forms*

There are many different forms these textual expressions can take. For example, if we turn to early phenomenological research following Dahlberg we would most likely see an essential meaning structure statement followed by a series of meaning patterns that, as a whole, constitute the essential meanings of the phenomenon. If we turn to a study following Van Manen's approach, we would most likely see essential themes without a central organizing meaning structure statement. I have done both and now feel that a central organizing statement does more centering than I would like, and it does not reflect the "tentative manifestation image" nor the "chasing lines of flight" heuristic previously described.

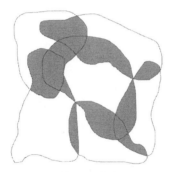

Figure 8.1

As an author of a post-intentional text, you should feel free to play with form, bringing all that you have from the data, your post-reflexion journal, other readings, other theories, and other philosophies to bear. I think the text can take many forms as long as it reads coherently, includes the identified tentative manifestations in some way, draws on philosophical conversation(s), is situated in the identified scholarly conversation(s) within particular fields, and reflects your post-reflexive work. Try to find a form that can reflect the tentative manifestation image. In other words write around and through the grey areas—whatever they might come to be—and amplify the explosive lines of flight.

With these points in mind, chapter 9 focuses on post-intentional phenomenology in practice.

Post-Intentional Phenomenology in Practice

The examples I have chosen to include here reflect some of the possible ways to craft post-intentional phenomenological texts. I say relatively little about each one, in large part because I want the texts to speak for themselves. That said, I do provide brief context leading into and out of each one, and in transition to the next. They are, because of space limitations of course, small excerpts from much larger texts. Please refer to the larger texts from which these excerpts are taken in order to get a better sense of the multiple, varied, and nuanced ways these post-intentional phenomenological crafts-women and men crafted their texts.

We begin with Dr. Joseph Pate's (2012) text, which as he writes, "leveraged Post-Intentional Phenomenology (Vagle 2010) to trouble, open up, and complexify understanding of the lived leisure experience (Parry and Johnson 2006) of connection with and through music listening" (p. 1). Pate opens his text with a prelude in which he not only invites the reader to the text and to the phenomenon, but also helps the reader begin to understand the importance of creating a collection of music.

PRELUDE
THERE'S A SECRET INSIDE AND A WHIRLPOOL OF EMOTIONS:
AN OPEN INVITATION TO THE READER-AS-LISTENER

For me it's huge—If I'm going to make a collection of music for someone, I'm going to be intentional about it. I'm not just going to randomly pull stuff, especially with something like this. I put thought into it and it's a part of me, it's a piece of who I am—each song has impacted me in some way. It might sound weird, but it's almost like every time I share it with someone else, I'm giving them a part of myself. I'm exposing myself a little bit more; I'm letting them have that insight into another layer of who I am. There's that trust and also that vulnerability at the same time—are they going to think this is lame or are they going to be like that was just "ok?" It's a sharing of a part of your soul with someone else, especially with pieces that have resonated with you in a deep way, in a lasting way.

Zoë,[1] Participant

An Open Invitation

There is an "art" to the creation of a good compilation[2] of music. It is a subtle art, which like many creative endeavors, arises from making intentional structural decisions to inform the larger, broader backdrop of purposeful and playful engagement with ideas and music through the expression and creation of diverse and varied, aurally-emotive experiences. Just as Nick Hornby indicated in *High Fidelity* (1995), "making a tape is like writing a letter—there is a lot of erasing and rethinking and starting again. A good compilation tape is hard to do. You have got to kick off with a corker, to hold the attention. Then ... up it a notch, or cool it a notch ... oh, there are loads of rules" (pp. 88–89). Creating compilations affords opportunities for a sonic collection of connection: connection to self, connection to lived-experiences, connection to others, and ...

As one continues through Pate's text one not only reads about the phenomenon, but has the opportunity to engage in and experience the phenomenon itself—for Pate created a compilation of music for his readers, a 13 track mix of various songs. He invites readers to listen to particular tracks as we read our way through his text. Here is one of my favorite stretches entitled, *Cairns and Echoes: The Lustering Potency of Song.*[3]

Joseph:[4] [*nervously fiddling on his computer*] I received an email the other day from one of my committee members.[5] He was in Spain and sent me a song, but he also troubled something that I was interested in getting your thoughts on. Here, let me find the email so I can get this right. Here it is: "The attached song has really hung with me lately. And I remember connecting with another Simply Red song called "Stars" from the early 90s (when I used to drive my son to high school). So I went back to it, and while I still like it a bit, it has lost its luster. As will this one in time. But for the moment, it grabs me." So, I was wondering: this lustering thing, what do you make of that?

Zoë: What do you mean by lustering?

Joseph: Yeah. What do I mean?

Zoë: I guess I think of gold having a luster. Maybe a shimmer? [*she said questioningly*]

Joseph: Yeah, I think that's probably the way it's being used here. Does that happen for you? Does a particular song, in certain moments have a certain shimmer, luster, or something which does something, and in other moments not?

Zoë: You know, it's weird. Now that I have been talking with you, I almost am looking for these moments with songs, and fascinatingly, they are not happening. Like I want them to happen so I can think about them, write about them, and tell you about them, but they are not happening right now. So, you want to know what I did last week? I listened to nothing. Driving, I just sat there in silence.

Joseph: So what happened?

Zoë: A couple days before we were to meet, I was randomly listening to something in the house, and bam, it was there. Isn't that how it always is? [*laughing*] It never happens when you are looking for it, and it comes when you're not?

Joseph: [*shifting forward in his chair*] So, when you were looking for it, did you listen to songs that you had had a moment of connection with in the past?

Zoë: Yeah, but that moment had gone. It had lost... [*pausing for a moment and looking over my shoulder outside*] Yeah, I guess you could say it had lost its luster. Or maybe potency is a better word. Like sometimes with perfume, if it is really strong and potent, you really recognize it, you know. But then, sometimes it is not, and it doesn't even register. It is weird. I will have a CD or be listening to my iPod and I just keep scrolling through all of these songs. Nothing is happening with any of them. And these are my songs! Songs I chose to buy, download, and create play lists.

As we can see from this example, Pate combines song—I listened to *Edge of Dream* and *Long Journey* as I wrote this—parts of his interview with a research participant—Zoë, and a footnote to craft this part of the text. The intertextual and intersubjective nature of this aspect of the text communicates through aesthetics, language, and emotion—making for powerful post-intentional engagement with the phenomenon.

I find these same qualities in the way Dr. Brooke Hofsess (2013b) crafts her text—in her case through letter-writing and visual art (printmaking). Throughout her entire text, the reader reads letters from Hofsess and between Hofsess and her research participants. Sometimes the letters focus on philosophy, other times methodological inquiry, and yet other times they represent "data." In all cases, readers are invited to the "swell," as Hofsess refers to it, of aesthetic experiential play—and I found (and continue to find) that if as a reader I allow myself to let go a bit more, I am able to ride the swells that Hofsess' text can take me on. Here is an example of a letter from early in the text.

Dear Reader,
   Playing around with a camera in the sun and in the low red glow of a high school darkroom at the age of seventeen set me free. Free to imagine myself becoming so many things. For a long time now, I have wanted to bestow this gift upon others. And I have been a dutiful and inspired teacher. And I would be lying if I said that I didn't sometimes miss that awakened place of artmaking, especially when I am too exhausted from teaching to make any work of my own. This longing led me back once more to join a circle

of learners—to ask new questions, to seek different answers, to understand more deeply the work of the artist-teacher. As one of my mentors wrote: "the continuous work we do on ourselves is a gift to those we teach."[6]

For seven years, I worked as a K-12 art teacher before leaving to become a teacher educator. It was bittersweet to leave, for I had come to see the art classroom as a space where time can be lost and attention to the present can be found through play and exploration. Busy things could be slowed down: by the sweeping motion of a paintbrush where blue meets green and becomes ocean; where the fusion of two pieces of clay between fingertips becomes vessel. As I began my dissertation research,[7] this intersection of play and aesthetic experience was the place where I began to wonder and write.

Yours,
Brooke

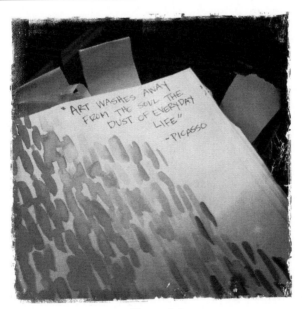

Figure 9.1

And here is an example of an image sent to research participants and a return letter that Hofsess received from one research participant.

March 25, 2012

Dear Brooke,
    I see the "dust" as all the stressors in life. I see art as a very emotional and expressive outlet and it is something someone can do to forget about their stressors and express any type of feeling through creating.

In my own creative practice, the visual journaling is a great exercise to "wash the dust off of my soul." This last month has been very stressful ... with grad school, wanting to find another job, but also wanting to stay at a job I love. I feel like I am going crazy at times! On top of all of that, I have been planning a school art show for our Related Arts night for a long time now, only to be told last week by a few of my teammates that we are not having a showcase after all—I am so disappointed! ALL of these things are driving me insane, but sitting down and working in my visual journal washes that dust away. I can take my frustration and create pieces that reflect my feelings. I can express them and many times by the end, I am feeling better and have come to the realization that everything will be okay. Art allows me to relax and let go (of) whatever it is that is bothering me on the inside. It has also made me want to fight for the hard work my students and I have put in. I have decided that I will be doing my own thing whether the other teachers want to or not. It may not be as big as I had envisioned it, but I promised the students and I won't let them down!

Our visit to the museum was great. I really appreciated the time you gave us. We went to the museum when we first started our graduate program, but it wasn't the same. Because we have come such a long way and have formed such good friendships, this experience meant incredibly more to me. I enjoyed working with a buddy and then coming together as a group to talk about what we saw—many times pointing out things that I would have otherwise missed. Our comfort with one another lends itself to a much more interesting and meaningful discussion, which we lacked in the beginning.

Sincerely,
Anne

And Hofsess' letter back to the participant.

April 4, 2012

Dear Anne,

I loved the way you opened your letter with the metaphor of dust as stress. As you wrote, the creative process often helps us deal with stress and feel more balanced, yet the more stressed out we get, the harder it is to create at all. What might be done about this for artist-teachers?

Your thoughts about the visual verbal journal as a place to work out the stress and dust resonated with me. I wonder, what is your favorite thing to do within the pages of your journal? Do you like to write or doodle? Make lists or ramble? What feels the most releasing of dust? Most liberating? Most daring? This may be something to consider thinking more deeply about for the final paper...

In addition to helping me see the dust as stress, you also have brought even closer to my attention, how the class community is working. We are so lucky to have such a tight knit group, where we can say and express without fear of rejection or critique.

Warmly,
Brooke
p.s. Best wishes for the art show!

Sometimes it is important, when crafting post-intentional phenomenological texts, to let entire excerpts and images be put in dialogue with other excerpts and images. And in doing so, allow the excerpts and images in their graphic proximity to speak for themselves. At times, in our attempts to be good researchers, we can weigh in too much. Hofsess' text reminds us that phenomena are often already telling us things that we do not need to analyze. Instead, as post-intentional phenomenological craftswomen and men, the choices we make to emphasize one thing or another—and knowing when to explain and when to get out of the text's way are critical.

I find Dr. Roberta Gardner's (2013) post-intentional phenomenological text strikes a beautiful balance among her interpretations, the voices of her participants, and images—all with the goal to "gain an understanding about living within and navigating a highly segregated hyper-racial space, specifically the ways in which Black youths and their parents absorbed the realities of being raced in their everyday lives and how these readings connect to their literacies" (p. 18).

Lighter and Brighter

Figure 9.2

I wanted the children to be aware that there were other choices for reading about Sojourner Truth, so I also used a book called *Step-Stomp Stride* (Pinkney & Pinkney, 2009). When I held up the copy of the book and explained that this was the same person, Katrina rolled her eyes and slapped her hand on the floor and shook her head as if she was truly grateful. "Gooood," she added drawing out her word, "Cause she look way more better in this one."

All of the children agreed with Katrina, but they did get plenty of digs in about Sojourner's "big old shoes." Da'veon yelped, "Look at them big ol' roach stompers." In *Step-Stomp Stride*, the overall aesthetic and feel of the book is lighter and less ominous than *Only Passing Through*. The focus is less on slavery and more on the speeches that she made about freedom and women's suffrage. Sojourner looks less "alien like" in *Stomp*; however, in this text, Sojourner's features are also abstracted. Her dark skin is a lighter pecan color. Her nose and lips are keener, more European looking, and unlike her actual physical traits. There is a sense of vibrancy, positivity, and sometimes a humorous tone. The water colors and brush strokes in *Stomp* are soft and brisk. Sojourner is rendered "large and in charge," but she is more stylized in her clothing than the version rendered by Rockwell and Christie. It has more kid appeal. For example, although she appears as somewhat of a messianic figure in both books, in *Stomp*, the rings of the sun form a variable halo around Sojourner's head as she "strides" "steps" and "stomps" toward justice. There is no sun in Rockwell and Christie's book, which is recommended for children ages 6 and up. In fact, when Rockwell does describe the sun, it is symbolic of her fateful entry into slavery when Sojourner is nine years old and is being auctioned off.

I wanted to get to these kinds of readings but we couldn't get past her unforgivable blackness. Conversely, in *Stomp*, readers feel a sense of warmth, energy, affirmation, beauty, and hope. Andrea Pinkney uses a poetic form to draw the reader into the text. It opens:

> She was big. She was black. She was *so* beautiful. Born into slavery, Belle had to endure the cruelty of several masters before she escaped to freedom. And oh, was freedom sweet!

The Pinkneys also demonstrate Sojourner's strength and determination through an effective pairing and synergy of the images and text (Sipe, 1998), but it's quite different from *Only Passing Through*. The book exudes power, but it also *feels good*. The lyrical flow of language and umber tones in swathes of buttery gold, sienna, and misty blue create a textual ecology (Lewis, 2001) that is captivating, inviting. An aurora—the uplift and dawning of a new day, can you feel it when you look at these pictures?

The kids genuinely liked the lyrical flow of this book, "That one is good." "I think I did this report on her with my partner in reading," "This one is nicer." This one is just better, cause I like the pictures. The kids generally absorbed the feel good message in *Stomp*, and they made connections back to school.

I read Gardner's post-intentional text, and this excerpt in particular, as a delicately woven tapestry—one in which the nuances are tightly woven, but not so tight that the unique fabric(s) are lost. I have found this difficult to do, and something Gardner does well. I also think Gardner has a unique and powerful way of bringing us to the phenomenon as it is lived by and with her participants. We can feel, sense, see, and almost be there with them.

And in the final example, we come to Dr. Hilary Hughes' (2011) multi-genre text—crafted in the form of a teen magazine. It contains a number of different genres, thus allowing the reader to engage on multiple levels and in multiple ways. Like Pate, Hofsess, and Gardner, Hughes does a masterful job making choices about what to say and not say in her crafting of the text. Focusing on the phenomenon of young adolescent girls' experiences of "bodily not-enoughness," Hughes found it necessary to let her young adolescent research participants take the lead in opening up the phenomenon. That is, when Hughes let go of trying to "interview" the girls, she learned a great deal about the phenomenon. In order to try to capture this within the phenomenon, Hughes crafted a multi-voiced, found poem in order to recapture a conversation she had with her participants at the pizza place. The language in the left column are from Hughes and the language in the right column represents the participants'—each indent signifies a different participant. I leave you with an excerpt from the poem Hughes (2011, 2012, pp. 98–99).

Look, pictures of you!	
	Oh, I hate that picture
	I look so fat
You're joking, right?	
	No
	I look so ugly
	I look
	I look
Who *ARE* You?	I look pale
	I like the second one
	I look like I'm only half of me
To the magazines then	
	J-14?
	But first I have to say something—
But not right now—	
I'm just sayin'	
we're not doing that right now	
... but ... go ahead—	
	They just need me all through
	this magazine
	I like that shirt: "mind, body, spirit"—
	we're going to be talking about our
	mind and our bodies
	Girls, I notice, are comfortable
	talking about their
	bodies
	around girls their age

Wait, what now?

I agree.

or like, someone they trust,
they know well

Girls, *most girls,* are comfortable
talking about their bodies around
girls
their age
or people they trust
or are close to
but no one else
like, seriously.
Or, older people who they trust.

Are we a sorority?
Are we the Purple Flowers sorority?

But we're really close
so we're OK with it—
But bring in somebody else
somebody who's not close—
it's like the conversation stops
and we're like, *Nice weather we're
having*

Resource Dig (Section 3)

Post-Intentional Phenomenology

Given that post-intentional phenomenology is a relatively "new" phenomenological approach, the resources are also quite recent and are mostly
doctoral dissertations, with a few articles as well. In addition to the examples provided in chapter 9, I list studies that have used centrally, or drew
upon, post-intentional phenomenological philosophies and methodologies.
Consistent with core commitments in post-intentional work, each of these
studies is unique in its focus and structure, and collectively live out the
tentative nature of various phenomena.

Post-Intentional Phenomenological Studies

Adams, M. G. "A Phenomenological Study of Adolescents' Perceptions of Empowerment"
(PhD diss., University of Georgia, 2012).

Benson, T. K. "A Post-Intentional Phenomenological Case Study of Pedagogical Awareness
of Technology Integration into Secondary Science Teaching" (PhD diss., University
of Minnesota, 2012).

Hofsess, B. 2013. "Methodology in the Afterglow." *International Journal of Education &
the Arts 14.*

Jersawitz, M. "Teenage Pregnancy: Societal Views as Seen Through Popular Film" (PhD
diss., University of Georgia, 2012).

Kumm, B. E. "A Shaman, a Sherpa, and a Healer: A Post-intentional Phenomenology of
Songwriting" (Masters Thesis, University of Georgia, 2011).

Kumm, B. E. 2013. "Finding healing through songwriting: A song for Nicolette." *International Journal of Community Music 6*(2):205–217.

Pate, J. A., and Johnson, C. W. 2013. "Sympathetic chords: Reverberating connection
through the lived leisure experiences of music listening." *International Journal of
Community Music 6*(2):189–203.

Pazurek, A. "A Phenomenological Investigation of Online Learners' Lived Experiences
of Engagement" (PhD diss., University of Minnesota, 2013).

Soule, K. "Connected: A Phenomenology of Attachment Parenting" (PhD diss., University
of Georgia, 2013).

Wells, S. "A Phenomenological Inquiry into being a Middle School Principal in a High
Stakes Testing Era" (PhD diss., University of Georgia, 2013).

Epilogue

I have never been good at good-byes.

I tend to either ramble on and on, repeating myself and incessantly over-processing information—or I end really abruptly, leaving people wondering what just happened.

I am not sure why I struggle to be more nuanced in my good-byes. It most likely stems from deep-seated issues from my childhood that a good phenomenological craftsperson could open up for consideration. However, I think I will save that analysis for another time and another place.

In my earlier drafts of this book, reviewers were consistent in suggesting that my closing—this epilogue—was way too short, too abrupt. They felt I needed to tie the book together more, leave the reader with some final, important ideas. Here is the closing-type language I had neatly tucked into the third resource dig.

I want to also the close the book with a few very short thoughts as you begin and/or continue to hone your craft.

Be open

Be patient

Be honest, yet gentle with yourself

Be serious, yet playful

Be contemplative, yet decisive

And most of all, be phenomenological

Happy crafting . . .

This is, indeed, a ridiculously short good-bye—especially considering all we have been through together.

As I re-read my original epilogue I laugh at my abruptness and, yet, am still drawn to the simplicity and underlying messages driving my "Be ..." statements. That said, the final, published epilogue does need more. What follows, then, is my attempt to split the difference between my over-processing good-bye motif and my abrupt good-bye motif. The first change I make is to move from "Be ..." statements to "Becoming ..." statements—in order to signal that we will never "arrive" but will be works in progress as we navigate contexts, situations, challenges, successes, and so on. The second change I make is to illustrate each statement through some of my own reflections and stories.

Becoming Open

This is really hard, yet is incredibly important when crafting phenomenological research. Moving from having to control, decide, and direct, to becoming open demands much from us. It might be useful to try to do something you are not good at. I am serious.

A few years back someone advised me to do this—he suggested that I might go take salsa dancing or pottery lessons. The goal would be to put myself in a highly vulnerable position so that I could experience the openness this vulnerability would demand. I kindly ignored his suggestion at the time, but later decided to try something else—Tae Kwon Do. I joined my two sons, Rhys (now nine years old) and Chase (now six years old), in taking lessons. Both of them were (and still are) much better than I. I felt quite vulnerable as I mis-stepped, kicked way lower than everyone else, and could not escape how I was a half-second behind the rest of the class when I looked in the mirror. I had to detach from my fears and emotions a bit, in order to learn and grow. It was good for me. You might consider the same.

Becoming Patient

Although patience and openness are related, I do not see them as one and the same. The ability to slow down and wait is unique. My earlier reference to *Peaceful Warrior*'s "there is never nothing going on" applies here, in that it demands a radical slowing down. I would like to take this a step further, though, and suggest that once we can learn to slow down more, we then can exercise a mindful patience for what might come next.

I remember transitioning from playing junior varsity to varsity football. When I first started to get significant playing time on the varsity team, the game seemed very fast. I felt like I could not keep up, not only because everyone seemed, and in many cases were, physically quicker and faster runners, but also because everyone seemed quicker and faster in their decision-making. However, as I played more the game seemed to slow down. One can hear football coaches and television analysts describe this rather odd phenomenon. The actual speed did not change, of course, but my experiencing of the speed did change. I would argue that I became more comfortable, present, and patient on the field.

When crafting phenomenological research, we need to slow down in this way. It is not as though we will not have deadlines, or that the actual time and timelines will change. It is how we experience our patient crafting over this time.

Becoming Honest, yet Gentle with Yourself

This is another tension to try to resolve. How might we be honest about our own successes and failures without overstating the positive and beating ourselves up for our failures. I have met folks who seem to be really good at this—and have been impressed by their consistency in this regard. The point I want emphasize most here is how we might proceed when something does not go as we had hoped or as we had planned. This is a particularly acute problem for those who suffer from perfectionism, and my guess is that many scholars do.

If we approach our crafting with the idea that we can do it perfectly, our crafting will most likely not turn out as powerful and creative as it could and will likely not be a very enjoyable experience. I suggest that we try to take a healthy, honest appraisal of when things go well, and when things do not—name them as such and then move on to our next opportunity to do better.

Becoming Serious, yet Playful

My son Chase is really good at this. Again, he is six. I continue to learn a lot from him. Recently, I needed to change our plans for going to a University of Minnesota home football game due to all sorts of conflicts. When he learned of this, Chase was extremely upset. After letting me know verbally how unjust my decision was, he stormed upstairs. About twenty minutes later he came downstairs and handed me a letter that read (his spellings, punctuation, and spacing preserved):

Dear Dad
I Luve
You I I m
Mad thet
I cudint
Cum to the
FetBoL
Gam
But I Stil
Luve you
And I hop
You hav
A Gud
Thxgiving
With me
And I will

Put my clous
on

I read this as a really positive way to communicate his disgust with me, to reconnect with me moving forward, and some comic relief at the end—for as Chase said to me later when we talked through the situation and the good writing he did in response, "it needed something funny."

Remember, the work we do is serious and important, but it is often wise to make some of it funny.

Becoming Contemplative, yet Decisive

Throughout this book, and again here, I have emphasized the importance of being contemplative in our crafting of phenomenological research. I want to also emphasize, though, the importance of making decisions. I have noticed sometimes that when I speak publicly about slowing down, practicing openness and patience, and contemplating, I get some quizzical looks and questions, often assuming that I am suggesting that phenomenologists just wait around, rather than take action. To the contrary, I think we need to be very decisive in our crafting, but not in a rushed or harried way. We need to become careful and thoughtful in our decision-making.

On one of my recent commutes to work, I heard something on morning talk radio that resonated with me. Mark Rosen, a widely respected sports anchor in Minneapolis-St. Paul, was discussing some of the important insights he had gained over his years in the business (it was Rosen's birthday). One of the most important insights he shared was something former Minnesota Vikings football coach and legend Bud Grant had told him. Grant had suggested to Rosen to "never make a decision before you have to" (M. Rosen, personal communication, 11/13/13).

I could not help but think about the same when crafting phenomenological research. You will need to make all sorts of decisions, but do not rush these decisions. Sit with ideas, situations, and possibilities for as long as you can, and then decide.

And Most of All, Becoming Phenomenological

This really involves all of the above as a cohesive whole, a blending of becomings that when combined can grow in their amplitude. Another way to conceive of this blended crafting, is to think of the work of building. I think builders are fascinating craftswomen and men. My stepmother's brother-in-law and nephew are builders. Although I have only worked with them once, I marveled at how they could visualize, plan, and enact what they wanted to build by looking at empty space. My son Rhys (again, nine) has this same gift. Since he was quite young he has been able to see what he wants to build in empty space. At six years old Rhys told me, "I just see it in my head," when I asked him how he made the structure in this picture.

Figure Ep.1

If you can continue to work on becoming open, patient, honest-yet gentle, serious-yet playful, and contemplative-yet decisive, I think you will *just see phenomenology in your head* and perhaps find yourself not only able to craft meaningful phenomenological research, but also content in doing so.

Happy Crafting ...

Additional Resources

Philosophically-Oriented

Websites

http://www.phenomenologycenter.org/
http://www.spep.org/
http://www.phenomenology.org/
http://www.phenomenologyresearchcenter.org/
http://institute.phenomenology.ro/en

Texts

Cerbone, D. R. 2008. *Heidegger: A guide for the perplexed.* New York: Continuum.

Dagenais, J. J. 1972. *Models of man: A phenomenological critique of some paradigms in the human sciences.* The Hague, Martinus Nijhoff.

Dilthey, W. 1923. *Introduction to the human sciences: An Attempt to lay a foundation for the study of society and history,* trans. R. J. Betanzos. Detroit, MI: Wayne State University Press.

Freeman, M. and M. D. Vagle. "Turning hermeneutics and phenomenology on one Another: Implications for qualitative research" (Paper presented at the annual meeting of the American Educational Research Association. San Diego, CA., April 2009).

Heidegger, M. 1982. *The basic problems of phenomenology,* trans. A. Hofstadter. Bloomington, IN: Indiana University Press.

Lawn, C. 2006. *Gadamer: A guide for the perplexed.* New York: Continuum.

Levinas, E. 1969. *Totality and infinity: An essay on exteriority,* trans. A. Lingis. Pittsburgh, PA: Duquesne University Press.

Levinas, E. 2002. "Beyond intentionality," in *The phenomenology reader,* eds. D. Moran and T. Mooney. New York, NY: Routledge.

Matthews, E. 2006. *Merleau-Ponty: A guide for the perplexed.* New York: Continuum.

Merleau-Ponty, M. 1964[1947]. *Primacy of perception: And other essays on phenomenological psychology, the philosophy of art, history and politics,* trans. J. Edie. Evanston, IL: Northwestern University Press.

Russell, M. 2006. *Husserl: A guide for the perplexed.* New York: Continuum.

Sartre, J. P. 2002[1939]. "Intentionality: A fundamental idea of Husserl's phenomenology," in *The Phenomenology Reader, eds.* D. Moran and T. Mooney. New York: Routledge.

Schutz, A. and T. Luckmann. 1973. *The structures of the life-world,* trans. R. M. Zaner and H. T. Engelhardt, Jr. Northwestern University Press: Evanston, IL.

Skirry, J. 2008. *Descartes: A guide for the perplexed.* New York: Continuum.

Methodologically-Oriented

Websites

http://phenomenology.utk.edu/default.html
http://www.phenomenologyonline.com/
http://www.maxvanmanen.com/
http://www.ipjp.org/index.php?option=com_contact&view=contact&id=29%3Aamed
   eo-giorgi&catid=4%3Aeditorialboard&Itemid=15
http://www.open.ac.uk/socialsciences/ihsrc2011/panel/#karin-dahlberg
http://www.lindafinlay.co.uk
http://www.nursingtimes.net/phenomenology-in-nursing-research-methodology-inter-
   viewing-and-transcribing/5005138.article

Texts

Nursing & Other Health–Related Fields

Annelis, M. 2006. "Hermeneutic phenomenology: Philosophical perspectives and current use in nursing research." *Journal of Advanced Nursing 23*(4):705–713.

Crotty. M. 1996. *Phenomenology and nursing research.* Churchill Livingstone: Melbourne, Australia.

Dahlberg, K. 2006b. "The publication of qualitative research findings." *Qualitative health research* 16(3):444–446.

McNamara, M.S. 2005. "Knowing and doing phenomenology: The implications of the critique of "nursing phenomenology" for a phenomenological inquiry: A discussion paper." *International Journal of Nursing Studies 42*:695–704.

Oiler, C. 1982. "The phenomenological approach in nursing research." *Nursing Research* 31: 178–181.

Education & Pedagogy

Amparo, R. F. 2013. "Gaining Insight into Teaching: A Phenomenological Exploration of the Lived Experience of the Teachers of the Year." FIU Electronic Theses and Dissertations. Paper 871. http://digitalcommons.fiu.edu/etd/871.

Greenwalt, K.A. 2008. "Through the camera's eye: A phenomenological analysis of teacher subjectivity." *Teaching and Teacher Education 24* (2):387–399.

Kim, J. 2012. "Understanding the lived experience of a Sioux Indian male adolescent: Toward the pedagogy of hermeneutical phenomenology in education." *Educational Philosophy and Theory, 44*(6):2012. doi: 10.1111/j.1469-5812.2010.00733.x.

Vagle, M. D. 2011. "Critically-oriented pedagogical tact: Learning about and through our compulsions as teacher educators." *Teaching Education, 22*(4):413–426.

Vagle, M. D. 2011. "Lessons in contingent, recursive humility." *Journal of Adolescent and Adult Literacy, 54*(6):362–370.

Vagle, M. D. 2009. "Locating and exploring teacher perception in the reflective thinking process." *Teachers and Teaching: Theory and Practice, 15*(5):579–599.

Vagle, M. D. 2006. "Dignity and democracy: An exploration of middle school teachers' pedagogy." *Research in Middle Level Education Online, 29*(8):1–17.

Communications

Langsdorf, L. 1994. "Why phenomenology in communication research?" *Human Studies, 17*:1–8.

Wood, D. nd. "Running in hermeneutic circles: A visual phenomenological methodology." Retrieved August 26, 2013 at http://www.academia.edu/1031177/Running_in_Hermeneutic_Circles_A_Visual_Phenomenological_Methodology.

Psychology

Colaizzi, P. 1978. "Psychological research as the phenomenologist views it," in *Existential-Phenomenological Alternatives for Psychology,* eds. R. Valle and M. King. New York: Oxford University Press.

Giorgi, A. 1970. *Psychology as a human science: A phenomenology-based approach.* New York: Harper & Row.

Giorgi, A. 1985. *Phenomenology and psychological research.* Pittsburgh: Duquesne University Press.

Giorgi, A. 1997. "The theory, practice, and evaluation of the phenomenological method as a qualitative research procedure." *Journal of Phenomenological Psychology, 28*(2):235–60.

van Kaam, A. 1966. *Existential foundations of psychology.* Pittsburgh: Dusquesne University Press.

Wertz, F. J. 2005. "Phenomenological research methods for counseling psychology." *Journal of Counseling Psychology,* 52(2):167–177.

Other Fields

Alvesson, M., C. Hardy, and B. Harley. 2008. "Reflecting on reflexivity: Reflexive textual practices in organization and management theory." *Journal of Management Studies,* 45(3):480–501.

Melrose, L. 1989. *The creative personality and the creative process: A phenomenological perspective.* Lanham, MD, University Press of America.

Thompson, C. J., W. B. Locander, et al. 1989. "Putting consumer experience back into consumer research: The philosophy and method of existential phenomenology." *Journal of Consumer Research,* 16(2):133–146.

Across Fields

Finlay, L. 2008b. "Introduction to phenomenology." Retrieved August 25, 2013 from http://www.lindafinlay.co.uk/phenomenology.htm.

Holstein, J. A. and J. F. Gubrium. 1998. "Phenomenology, ethnomethodology, and interpretive practice," in *Strategies of qualitative inquiry,* eds. N. K. Denzin and Y. S. Lincoln. Thousand Oaks, CA, Sage.

Kvale, S. 1983. "The qualitative research interview: A phenomenological and a hermeneutical mode of understanding." *Journal of Phenomenological Psychology* 14(2):171–196.

Woolgar, S. 1988. "Reflexivity is the ethnographer of the text," in *Knowledge and reflexivity: New frontiers in the sociology of knowledge,* ed. S. Woolgar. Newbury Park, CA: Sage.

Post-Intentional Studies

Gardner, R. "Reading race in a community space: A narrative post-intentional phenomenological exploration" (PhD diss., University of Georgia, 2013).

Hofsess, B. "Embodied intensities: Artist-teacher renewal in the swell and afterglow of aesthetic experiential play" (PhD diss., University of Georgia, 2013).

Hughes, H. E. "Phenomenal bodies, phenomenal girls: How young adolescent girls experience being enough in their bodies" (PhD diss., University of Georgia, 2011).

Pate, J. "A Space for Connection: A Phenomenological Inquiry on Music Listening as Leisure" (PhD diss., University of Georgia, 2012).

Resources that Draw on Post-Intentional Ideas

Abrahamson, D. "Toward a Taxonomy of Design Genres: Fostering Mathematical Insight via Perception-Based and Action-Based Experiences" (Paper presented at the Proceedings of the 12th Annual Interaction Design and Children Conference, IDC 2013).

Abrahamson, D. 2012. "Seeing chance: perceptual reasoning as an epistemic resource for grounding compound event spaces." *ZDM Mathematics Education, 44*(7):869–881.

Hofsess, B. A., and J. L. Sonenberg. 2013. "Enter: Ho/rhizoanalysis." *Cultural Studies Critical Methodologies.* Online version, doi: 10.1177/1532708613487877.

Ojala, M., and T. Venninen. 2011. "Developing reflective practices for day-care centres in the Helsinki Metropolitan Area." *Reflective Practice, 12*(3):335–346.

Shaw, R. "The boundaries of time: Heidegger's phenomenology of time as the precursor of a new pedagogy" (Paper presented at the Philosophy of Education Society of Australasia, 2012).

Thiel, J. J. 2013. "The audacity of building community: a teacher looks at the end of every fork." *Teaching Education 24*(3): 292-301.

Notes

Chapter One

1. I discuss the egocentric predicament a number of times throughout this volume.
2. I too come from a working-class upbringing. Although this book is not an attempt to produce theories concerning social class, I think my growing craft is deeply connected to my working-class roots. Moreover, a significant part of my scholarship focuses on social class and education (see Jones and Vagle 2013; Vagle and Jones 2012).

Chapter Two

1. I say a bit more here about how intentionality is conceived in my post-intentional approach—not because Husserlian and Heideggerian conceptions are simpler. Rather, it is because the post-intentional is much newer, departs a bit from the former, and therefore requires a bit more background and explanation.
2. I would like to thank Mr. Troy Bassett for creating *the essential core and tentative manifestations* computerized figures and Ms. Keri Valentine for creating the *hermeneutic spiral* computerized figure.

Chapter Three

1. In fact, you can see my struggle with drawing lines between phenomenological approaches fairly early in my growing craft. I write about it some in my dissertation (Vagle 2006) and explicitly in a piece published in the International Journal of Qualitative Studies in Education (Vagle 2009).

Chapter Four

1. There are a number of other high-amplitude possibilities that one might find helpful as well—Moustakas (1994), Pollio, Henley, and Thompson (2006), and Smith, Flowers, and Larkin (2009), to name three. In addition, one can find more resources in the resource dig.

Chapter Five

1. In section 3 I extend the idea of bridling to what I am calling "post-reflexivity" in "post-intentional phenomenology."
2. I learned of these considerations from Dr. Julie Kalnin during my doctoral studies.

Chapter Six

1. Please keep in mind that these rules are more generally an excellent practical way to move from the natural to the phenomenological attitude when observing, writing, reading, thinking, dancing, drawing, about and with phenomena.
2. See Adams (2012) for a deeper discussion of how Heidegger's conception informed her study and what she learned.

Chapter Seven

1. I use the terms "old" and "new" as an extension of Ihde's (2003) distinction between an old subject-centered phenomenology and a postphenomenology.
2. My thanks to Joseph Pate for sending Ihde's work my way.
3. I have served as lead author on two other papers (Vagle et al. 2013, Vagle and Hofsess 2014) in which we also theorize lines of flight.

Chapter Eight

1. I use much of the same theoretical and methodological set-up in Vagle (2010a) that I do here.
2. The notion of post-reflexivity that I describe in the next few pages was first introduced in a co-authored paper (Vagle, Monette, Thiel, and Wester-Neal 2013, under review).
3. Operationalizing Deleuze and Guattari's lines of flight (for different purposes than I do here) was first introduced in papers I wrote with Rachel Monette, Jaye Thiel, and Katie Wester-Neal and Brooke Hofsess, respectively. Those papers were presented at AERA 2013 (the first) and AERA 2014 (the second, with Hofsess) and are now being submitted for journal review.

Chapter Nine

1. Each participant suggested a pseudonym for use in analysis and presentation of the data. All participant "talk" was edited for readability. For example, "filler words" were removed, grammar corrected for discursive representation, and pronouns changed to be in agreement with the constructed text. I elected to block quote and italicize the majority of participant talk in consideration of constructing a polyvocal text (described more fully below). Further, in certain circumstances I included specific exchanges from the interviews that more fully revealed and opened up the phenomenon or demonstrated the evolving and iterative nature of understanding which emerged by including my presence and questions as part of the lifted text. Finally, in consideration of my authorial presence, I attempted to remain true to my participant's words, thoughts, and the presentation of those words and thoughts.
2. Compilations are and were created through many different forms: audio cassette tapes, CDs, playlists. Compilations are also known as mix/mixes. Please read "compilations" broadly and interchangeably.
3. Tracks 10 and 11, *Long Journey* and *Edge of a Dream*, by Sarah Jarosz (2009b & 2009a) are associated with this tentative manifestation.
4. This final tentative manifestation took up the call forwarded by Parry and Johnson (2006) for creative analytical practices (CAP) to address lived leisure experiences, revealing their complexity and opening up how an activity that may be understood as leisure is experienced, studied, presented, and understood. Arguably, this whole polyvocal text attempted to achieve this undertaking. For this specific manifestation, a constructed narrative account in the form of a dialogue is presented between myself and Zoe, leveraging the metaphors of cairns and echoes to reveal the fluid and dynamic lustering potency of song. The majority of this dialogue is directly pulled from Zoe's transcripts, although some ideas come from the other participants and was used for conventions in literary works. I encourage you as the reader-as-listener to read this out loud, evoking Ihde's (2007) idea that hearing can engage us in multiple ways of "knowing." Through this manifestation, I hope to encourage new understandings and reveal the complexity of this lived leisure

experience, which exists at the heart of Creative Analytical Practice (Parry and Johnson 2007; Richardson and St. Pierre 2005).

5. Thank you to Dr. Douglas Kleiber for continually sending me these thought provoking "nuggets," even across the big pond.

6. Vagle, M. D. 2010b. "Post-intentional Phenomenological Research Approach" (Paper presented at the Annual Meeting of the *American Educational Research Association,* San Francisco, California, p. 424).

7. Some of this text was reworked from an earlier publication; *see* Hofsess, B. 2013a. "Methodology in the Afterglow." *International Journal of Education & the Arts 14*(1.8):1–22.

References

Abrahamson, D. "Toward a Taxonomy of Design Genres: Fostering Mathematical Insight via Perception-Based and Action-Based Experiences" (Paper presented at the Proceedings of the 12th Annual Interaction Design and Children Conference, IDC 2013).

Abrahamson, D. 2012. "Seeing chance: perceptual reasoning as an epistemic resource for grounding compound event spaces." *ZDM Mathematics Education, 44*(7):869–881.

Adams, M. G. "A Phenomenological Study of Adolescents' Perceptions of Empowerment" (PhD diss., University of Georgia, 2012).

Ahmed, S. 2006. *Queer phenomenology: Orientations, objects, others.* Durham, NC: Duke University Press.

Alvesson, M., C. Hardy, and B. Harley. 2008. "Reflecting on reflexivity: Reflexive textual practices in organization and management theory." *Journal of Management Studies* 45 (3):480–501.

Amparo, R. F. 2013. "Gaining Insight into Teaching: A Phenomenological Exploration of the Lived Experience of the Teachers of the Year." FIU Electronic Theses and Dissertations. Paper 871. http://digitalcommons.fiu.edu/etd/871.

Annelis, M. 2006. "Hermeneutic phenomenology: Philosophical perspectives and current use in nursing research." *Journal of Advanced Nursing 23*(4):705–713.

Aronowitz, S. 2008. *Against schooling: For an education that matters.* Boulder, CO: Paradigm Publishers.

Benson, T. K. "A Post-Intentional Phenomenological Case Study of Pedagogical Awareness of Technology Integration into Secondary Science Teaching" (PhD diss., University of Minnesota, 2012).

Berliner, D. C. 2005. "Our impoverished view of educational reform." *Teachers College Record.* Retrieved September 27, 2011 from http://www.tcrecord.org/content.asp?contentid=12106.

Berliner, D.C. 2006. "Our impoverished view of educational research." *Teachers College Record* 108:949–995.

Buckley, R.P. 1992. *Husserl, Heidegger, and the crisis of philosophical responsibility.* Norwel, MA: Kluwer Academic Publishers Group.

Butler-Kisber, L. 2010. *Qualitative inquiry: Thematic, narrative, and arts-informed perspectives.* Thousand Oaks, CA: Sage.

Carlsson, G., K. Dahlberg, K. Lutzen, and M. Nystrom. 2004. "Violent encounters in psychiatric care: A phenomenological study of embodied caring knowledge." *Issues in Mental Health Nursing* 25(2):191–217.

Cahnmann-Taylor, M. and R. Siegsemund. 2008. *Arts-based research in education: Foundations for practice.* New York: Routledge.

Cerbone, D. R. 2008. *Heidegger: A guide for the perplexed.* New York: Continuum.

Christian, J. L. 1994. *Philosophy: An introduction to the art of wondering, 6th ed.* Forth Worth, TX: Harcourt Brace College Publishers.

Colaizzi, P., 1978. "Psychological research as the phenomenologist views it." In *Existential-Phenomenological alternatives for psychology,* eds. R. Valle and M. King, New York: Oxford University Press: 48-71.

Crawford, M.B. 2011. *The case for working with your hands, or, why office work is bad for us and making things feels good.* New York: Penguin Viking.

Crotty. M. 1996. *Phenomenology and nursing research.* Melbourne, Australia: Churchill Livingstone.

Crotty, M. 2003. *The foundations of social research: Meaning and perspective in the research process*. Los Angeles, CA: Sage Publications.

Creswell, J. W. 2008. *Research design: Qualitative, quantitative, and mixed methods approaches*. Thousand Oaks, CA: Sage Publications, Inc.

Dagenais, J. J. 1972. *Models of man: A phenomenological critique of some paradigms in the human sciences*. The Hague, Martinus Nijhoff.

Dahlberg, H. and K. Dahlberg. 2003. "To not make definite what is indefinite. A phenomenological analysis of perception and its epistemological consequences." *Journal of the Humanistic Psychologist*, 31(4):34–50.

Dahlberg, K. 2006. "The essence of essences—The search for meaning structures in phenomenological analysis of lifeworld phenomena." *International journal of qualitative studies on health and well-being 1*:11–19.

Dahlberg, K. 2006b. "The publication of qualitative research findings." *Qualitative health research* 16(3):444–446.

Dahlberg, K., H. Dahlberg, and M. Nystrom. 2008. *Reflective lifeworld research*. (2nd ed). Lund, Sweden: Studentlitteratur.

Dahlberg, K., N. Drew, and M. Nystrom. 2001. *Reflective lifeworld research*. Lund, Sweden: Studentlitteratur.

Davies, B., and S. Gannon. 2006. *Doing collective biography*. New York: Open University Press.

Deleuze, G., and F. Guattari. 1987. *A thousand plateaus: Capitalism and schizophrenia*, trans. B. Massumi. Minneapolis: University of Minnesota Press.

Dilthey, W. 1923. *Introduction to the human sciences: An Attempt to lay a foundation for the study of society and history*, trans. R. J. Betanzos. Detroit, MI: Wayne State University Press.

Faux, J. 2012. *The servant economy: Where America's elite is sending the middle class*. (Hoboken, NJ: Wiley.

Feldman, A. 2003. "Validity and quality in self-study." *Educational Researcher* 32:26–28.

Fey, T. 2011. *Bossypants*. New York: Reagan Arthur Books/Little, Brown and Company—Hachette Book Group.

Finlay, L. 2008a. "A dance between the reduction and reflexivity: Explicating the phenomenological psychological attitude." *Journal of Phenomenological Psychology 39*:1–32.

Finlay, L. 2008b. "Introduction to phenomenology." Retrieved August 25, 2013 from http://www.lindafinlay.co.uk/phenomenology.htm.

Foucault, M. 1994. *The order of things: An archaeology of the human sciences*. New York: Vintage Books.

Freeman, M., K. deMarrais, J. Preissle, K. Roulston, and E. A. St. Pierre. 2007. "Standards of evidence in qualitative research: An incitement to discourse." *Educational Researcher* 36(1):25–32.

Freeman, M. and M. D. Vagle. "Turning hermeneutics and phenomenology on one Another: Implications for qualitative research" (Paper presented at the annual meeting of the American Educational Research Association. San Diego, CA., April 2009).

Freeman, M. and M. D. Vagle. 2013. "Grafting the intentional relation of hermeneutics and phenomenology in linguisticality." *Qualitative Inquiry 19*(9):725–735.

Gadamer, H-G. 1975. *Truth and method*. New York: Continuum.

Gardner, R. "Reading race in a community space: A narrative post-intentional phenomenological exploration" (PhD diss., University of Georgia, 2013).

Gladwell, M. 2009. *What the dog saw*. New York: Little, Brown & Company.

Giorgi, A. 1970. *Psychology as a human science: A phenomenology-based approach*. New York: Harper & Row.

Giorgi, A. 1985. *Phenomenology and psychological research*. Pittsburgh: Duquesne University Press.

Giorgi, A. 1997. "The theory, practice, and evaluation of the phenomenological method as a qualitative research procedure." *Journal of Phenomenological Psychology 28*(2):235–60.

Giorgi, A. 2005. "The phenomenological movement and research in the human sciences." *Nursing Science Quarterly* 18(1):75–82.

Giorgi, A. 2009. *The descriptive phenomenological method in psychology: A modified Husserlian approach.* Pittsburgh, PA: Duquesne University Press.

Greenwalt, K.A. 2008. "Through the camera's eye: A phenomenological analysis of teacher subjectivity." *Teaching and Teacher Education 24* (2):387–399.

Grondin, J. 2003. *Le tournant herméneutique de la phenomenology.* Paris, France: Presses Universitaires de France.

Grumet. M. 1988. *Bitter milk: Women and teaching.* Amherst, MA: The University of Massachusetts Press.

Heidegger, M. 1982. *The basic problems of phenomenology,* trans. A. Hofstadter. Blooming-ton, IN: Indiana University Press.

Heiddegger, M. 1998 [1927]. *Being and time, trans.* J. Macquarrie and E. Robinson. Oxford: Blackwells.

Heidegger, M. 2002a. "Hermeneutical phenomenology and fundamental ontology," in *The phenomenology reader,* eds. D. Moran, and T. Mooney. New York, NY: Routledge.

Heidegger, M. 2002b. "The phenomenological method of investigation," in *The phenom-enology reader,* eds. D. Moran, and T. Mooney. New York, NY: Routledge.

Heidegger, M. 2002c. "The worldhood of the world," in *The phenomenology reader,* eds. D. Moran, and T. Mooney. New York, NY: Routledge.

Hetland, L., E. Winner, S. Veenema, and K. Sheridan. 2007. *Studio thinking: The real benefits of visual arts education.* New York: Teachers College Press.

Hofsess, B. 2013a. "Methodology in the Afterglow." *International Journal of Education & the Arts 14*(1.8): 1-22.

Hofsess, B. "Embodied intensities: Artist-teacher renewal in the swell and afterglow of aesthetic experiential play" (PhD diss., University of Georgia, 2013b).

Hofsess, B. A., and J. L. Sonenberg. 2013. "Enter: Ho/rhizoanalysis." *Cultural Studies Critical Methodologies.* Online version, doi: 10.1177/1532708613487877.

Holstein, J. A. and J. F. Gubrium. 1998. "Phenomenology, ethnomethodology, and in-terpretive practice," in *Strategies of qualitative inquiry,* eds. N. K. Denzin and Y. S. Lincoln. Thousand Oaks, CA, Sage.

Hughes, H. E. "Phenomenal bodies, phenomenal girls: How young adolescent girls experience being enough in their bodies" (PhD diss., University of Georgia, 2011).

Hughes-Decatur, H. E., 2012. "Always becoming, never enough: Middle school girls talk back," in *Not a stage! A critical re-conception of young adolescent education,* ed. M. D. Vagle. New York, Peter Lang.

Husserl, E. 1970 [1936]. *The crisis of European sciences and transcendental phenomenology,* trans. D. Carr. Evanston, IL: Northwestern University Press.

Ihde, D., 1993. *Postphenomenology: Essays in the postmodern context.* Evanston, Il: North-western University Press.

Ihde, D. 2003. "Postphenomenology—again?" Working papers from Centre for STS Studies. Retrieved May 19, 2011 from http://sts.imv.au.dk/search/search_files_di-rectories/Ihde.

Jarosz, S. 2009a. Edge of a Dream [Recorded by Sarah Jarosz]. On *Song Up in Her Head* [CD]. United States: Sugar Hill Records.

Jarosz, S. 2009b. Long Journey [Recorded by Sarah Jarosz]. On *Song Up in Her Head* [CD]. United States: Sugar Hill Records.

Jersawitz, M. "Teenage Pregnancy: Societal Views as Seen Through Popular Film" (PhD diss., University of Georgia, 2012).

Jones, S., and M. D. Vagle. 2013. "Living contradictions and working for change: Toward a theory of social class-sensitive pedagogy." *Educational Researcher* 42(3):129–141.

Kim, J. 2012. "Understanding the lived experience of a Sioux Indian male adolescent: Toward the pedagogy of hermeneutical phenomenology in education." *Educational Philosophy and Theory, 44*(6):2012. doi: 10.1111/j.1469-5812.2010.00733.x.

Kumm, B. E. "A Shaman, a Sherpa, and a Healer: A Post-intentional Phenomenology of Songwriting" (Masters thesis, University of Georgia, 2011).

Kumm, B. E. 2013. "Finding healing through songwriting: A song for Nicolette." *International Journal of Community Music* 6(2):205–217.

Kvale, S. 1983. "The qualitative research interview: A phenomenological and a hermeneutical mode of understanding." *Journal of Phenomenological Psychology* 14(2):171–196.

Kvale, S., ed. 1989. *Issues of validity in qualitative research.* Lund: Studentlitteratur.

Kvale, S. 1995. "The social construction of validity." *Qualitative Inquiry* 1:19–40.

Langsdorf, L. 1994. "Why phenomenology in communication research?" *Human Studies,* 17:1–8.

Lather, P. 1993. "Fertile obsession: Validity after poststructularism." *Sociological Quarterly* 34(4):673–693.

Lather, P. 2001. "Validity as an incitement to discourse: Qualitative research and the crisis of legitimation," in *Handbook of research on teaching*, ed. V. Richardson. Washington, DC: American Educational Research Association.

Lather, P., and C. Smithies. 1997. *Troubling the angels: Women living with HIV/AIDS.* Boulder, CO: Westview Press.

Lawn, C. 2006. *Gadamer: A guide for the perplexed.* New York: Continuum.

LeCompte, M. D., and J. P. Goetz. 1982. "Problems of reliability and validity in ethnographic research." *Review of Educational Research,* 52(1):31–60.

Levinas, E. 1969. *Totality and infinity: An essay on exteriority,* trans. A. Lingis. Pittsburgh, PA: Duquesne University Press.

Levinas, E. 2002. "Beyond intentionality," in *The phenomenology reader,* eds. D. Moran and T. Mooney. New York, NY: Routledge.

Lincoln, Y. S. 1995. "Emerging criteria for quality in qualitative and interpretive research." *Qualitative Inquiry* 1:275–289.

Lorraine, T. 2005. "Lines of flight," in *The Deleuze dictionary,* ed. A. Parr. Edinburgh: Edinburg University Press.

Macbeth, D. 2001. "On 'reflexivity' in qualitative research: Two readings, and a third." *Qualitative Inquiry* 7(1):35–68.

Marquez-Zenkov, K. 2007. "Through city students' eyes: Urban students' beliefs about school's purposes, supports, and impediments." *Visual Studies* 22(2):138–154.

Matthews, E. 2006. *Merleau-Ponty: A guide for the perplexed.* New York: Continuum.

McNamara, M. S., 2005. "Knowing and doing phenomenology: The implications of the critique of 'nursing phenomenology' for a phenomenological inquiry: A discussion paper." *International Journal of Nursing Studies* 42:695–704.

Melrose, L. 1989. *The creative personality and the creative process: A phenomenological perspective.* Lanham, MD, University Press of America.

Merleau-Ponty, M. 1964[1947]. *Primacy of perception: And other essays on phenomenological psychology, the philosophy of art, history and politics,* trans. J. Edie. Evanston, IL: Northwestern University Press.

Merleau-Ponty, M. 1995 [1945]. *Phenomenology of perception,* trans. C. Smith. London, Routledge Classics.

Miles, M. B., and A. M. Huberman. 1984. "Drawing valid meaning from qualitative data: Toward a shared craft." *Educational Researcher* 13:20–30.

Moran, D. 2000. *Introduction to phenomenology*. Routledge, New York.

Moran, D., and T. Mooney, eds. 2002. *The phenomenology reader*, New York, NY: Routledge.

Morse, J., and S. E. Chung. 2003. "Toward holism: The significance of methodological pluralism." *International journal of qualitative methods, 2*(3):13–20.

Moustakas, C. 1994. *Phenomenological research methods*. Thousand Oaks, CA, Sage Publications.

Oiler, C. 1982. "The phenomenological approach in nursing research." *Nursing Research* 31: 178–181.

Ojala, M., and T. Venninen. 2011. "Developing reflective practices for day-care centres in the Helsinki Metropolitan Area." *Reflective Practice, 12*(3):335–346.

Parry, D. C., and C. W. Johnson. 2006. "Contextualizing leisure research to encompass complexity in lived leisure experience: The need for creative analytic practice." *Leisure Sciences* 29:119–130.

Pate, J. "A Space for Connection: A Phenomenological Inquiry on Music Listening as Leisure" (PhD diss., University of Georgia, 2012).

Pate, J. A., and Johnson, C. W. 2013. "Sympathetic chords: Reverberating connection through the lived leisure experiences of music listening." *International Journal of Community Music 6*(2):189–203.

Pazurek, A. "A Phenomenological Investigation of Online Learners' Lived Experiences of Engagement" (PhD diss., University of Minnesota, 2013).

Perri, C. 2010. *Jar of hearts*, producer Barrett Yeretsian.

Pinkney, A. D. and J.B. Pinkney (2009). *Sojourner Truth's step-stomp stride*. New York: Disney.

Pollio, H., T. B. Henley, and C. J. Thompson. 2006. *The phenomenology of everyday life*. New York: Cambridge University Press.

Raggl, A., and M. Schratz. 2004. "Using visuals to release pupil's voices: Emotional pathways to enhancing thinking and reflecting on learning," in *Seeing is believing? Approaches to visual research, Vol. 7*, ed. C. Pole. New York: Elsevier.

Reardon, S. F. 2011. "The widening achievement gap between the rich and the poor: New evidence and possible explanations," in *Whither opportunity? Rising inequality, schools, and children's life chances*, eds. G. Duncan and R. Murnane. New York: Russell Sage Foundation.

Reay, D. "On the wild side: Identifications and disidentifications in the Research field" (Paper presented at the Centre for Psycho-Social Studies. University of the West of England, 2004/5).

Reseapro 2013. "Research methods vs. research methodology." Retrieved August 3, 2013 at http://blog.reseapro.com/2012/05/research-methods-vs-research-methodology/.

Ritchie, S. M., and D. L. Rigano. 2001. "Researcher–participant positioning in classroom research." *International Journal of Qualitative Studies in Education* 14(6):741–756.

Rose, M. 1989. *Lives on the boundary: A moving account of the struggles and achievements of America's educationally underprepared*. New York: Penguin.

Rose, M. 2005. *The mind at work: Valuing the intelligence of the American worker*. New York: Penguin.

Rosen, M. personal communication, 11/13/13.

Rothstein, R. 2004. *Class and schools: Using social, economic, and educational reform to close the black-white achievement gap*. New York: Teachers College Press.

Russell, M. 2006. *Husserl: A guide for the perplexed*. New York: Continuum.

Salva, V., director, and K. Bernhardt, screenwriter. 2006. *Peaceful warrior*. Santa Monica: Lionsgate Films.

Sartre, J.-P. 2002[1939]. "Intentionality: A fundamental idea of Husserl's phenomenology," in *The Phenomenology Reader*, eds. D. Moran and T. Mooney. New York: Routledge.

Schutz, A. and T. Luckmann. 1973. *The structures of the life-world*, trans. R. M. Zaner and H. T. Engelhardt, Jr. Northwestern University Press: Evanston, IL.

Sartre, J.-P. 1943. *Being and nothingness: A phenomenological essay on ontology*, trans. H. E. Barnes. New York: Washington Square Press.

Schutz, A. 1967. *The phenomenology of the social world*, trans. G. Walsh and F. Lehnert. Evanston, IL: Northwestern University Press.

Scheurich, J. J. 1993. "The masks of validity: A deconstructive investigation." *International Journal of Qualitative Studies in Education* 9(11):49–60.

Scheurich, J. J. 1997. *Research method in the postmodern*. London, Falmer Press.

Shaw, R.. "The boundaries of time: Heidegger's phenomenology of time as the precursor of a new pedagogy" (Paper presented at the Philosophy of Education Society of Australasia, 2012).

Sipe, L.R. 1998. "How picture books work: A semiotically framed theory of text-picture relationships." *Children's Literature in Education, 29:* 97-108.

Skirry, J. 2008. *Descartes: A guide for the perplexed*. New York: Continuum.

Smith, J. A., P. Flowers, and M. Larkin. 2009. *Interpretive phenomenological analysis: Theory, method, and research*. London: Sage.

Sokolowski, R. 2000. *Introduction to phenomenology*. New York: Cambridge University Press.

Soule, K. "Connected: A Phenomenology of Attachment Parenting" (PhD diss., University of Georgia, 2013).

St.Pierre, E. A. 1997. "Nomadic inquiry in the smooth spaces of the field: A preface." *International Journal of Qualitative Studies in Education* 10(3):365–383.

Thiel, J. J. 2013. "The audacity of building community: a teacher looks at the end of every fork." *Teaching Education* 24(3): 292-301.

Thompson, C. J., W. B. Locander, et al. 1989. "Putting consumer experience back into consumer research: The philosophy and method of existential phenomenology." *Journal of Consumer Research, 16*(2):133–146.

Vagle, M. D. 2006. "Dignity and democracy: An exploration of middle school teachers' pedagogy." *Research in Middle Level Education Online, 29*(8):1–17.

Vagle, M. D. 2009. "Validity as intended: 'Bursting forth toward' bridling in phenomenological research." *International Journal of Qualitative Studies in Education* 22(5):585–605.

Vagle, M. D. 2009. "Locating and exploring teacher perception in the reflective thinking process." *Teachers and Teaching: Theory and Practice, 15*(5):579–599.

Vagle, M. D. 2010a. "Re-framing Schön's call for a phenomenology of practice: A post-intentional approach." *Reflective Practice: International and Multidisciplinary Perspectives 11*(3):393–407.

Vagle, M. D. "A post-intentional phenomenological research approach" (Paper presented at the annual meeting of the American Educational Research Association, Denver, CO, 2010, May).

Vagle, M. D. "Making a case for phenomenological literacy research" (Paper presented at the annual meeting of the Literacy Research Association [formerly National Reading Conference], Dallas-Fort Worth, TX, 2010, December).

Vagle, M. D. 2011. "Lessons in contingent, recursive humility." *Journal of Adolescent and Adult Literacy 54*(6):362–370.

Vagle, M. D. 2011. "Critically-oriented pedagogical tact: Learning about and through our compulsions as teacher educators." *Teaching Education, 22*(4):413–426.

Vagle, M. D., H. E. Hughes, and D. J. Durbin. 2009. "Remaining skeptical: Bridling for and with one another." *Field Methods* 21(4):347–367.

Vagle, M. D., R. Monette, J. Thiel, and K. Wester-Neal. "Trying to educate the bridling practitioner" (Paper presented at the Annual Meeting of the *American Educational Research Association*. San Francisco, California, 2013, May).

Vagle. M. D., and B. Hofsess. "Amplifying the post in post-intentional phenomenology"

(Paper presented at the Annual Meeting of the *American Educational Research Association*. Philadelphia, Pennsylvania, 2014).

van Kaam, A. 1966. *Existential foundations of psychology*. Pittsburgh, PA: Dusquesne University Press.

van Manen, M. 2001. *Researching lived experience*: *Human science for an action sensitive pedagogy*. Althouse Press: London: Ontario, Canada.

van Manen, M. 2013. "Phenomenologyonline: A resource for phenomenological inquiry." Retrieved August 27, 2013 at http://www.phenomenologyonline.com/inquiry/methods-procedures/empirical- methods/interviewing-experiences/.

van Manen, M. 2014. *Phenomenology of practice: Meaning-giving methods in phenomenological research and writing*. Thousand Oaks, CA: Left Coast Press.

Weitz, P., director, and K. Croner, screenwriter. 2013. *Admission*. Beverly Hills: Imagine Entertainment.

Wertz, F. J. 2005. "Phenomenological research methods for counseling psychology." *Journal of Counseling Psychology*, 52(2):167–177.

Wells, S. "A Phenomenological Inquiry into being a Middle School Principal in a High Stakes Testing Era" (PhD diss., University of Georgia, 2013).

Wood, D. nd. "Running in hermeneutic circles: A visual phenomenological methodology." Retrieved August 26, 2013 at http://www.academia.edu/1031177/Running_in_Hermeneutic_Circles_A_Visual_Phenomenological_Methodology.

Woolgar, S. 1988. "Reflexivity is the ethnographer of the text," in *Knowledge and reflexivity: New frontiers in the sociology of knowledge*, ed. S. Woolgar, 14–36. Newbury Park, CA: Sage.

Index

About the Author

Mark D. Vagle is Associate Professor of Curriculum and Instruction at the University of Minnesota. He has written extensively on phenomenological research in journals such as *Qualitative Inquiry, The International Journal of Qualitative Studies in Education, Field Methods, and Teaching Education,* and regularly teaches university courses and professional workshops on the subject. Vagle is principal author and editor of *Not a Stage! A Critical Re-Conception of Young Adolescent Education* and coeditor of *Developmentalism in Early Childhood and Middle Grades Education: A Critical Conversation on Readiness and Responsiveness.* Currently, Vagle is using his conception of post-intentional phenomenology to critically examine various ways in which issues related to social class take concrete (lived) shape in the curriculum and pedagogies of elementary education.